CHAMP
THE HUMAN
WHISPERER

Also by Dr. Harmony:

Twin Flame Code Breaker: 11 Key Codes
(English & Spanish Editions)

Twin Flame Ascension™: Take Me Home Oracle Deck

www.TwinFlameExpert.com

www.SoulWritersAcademy.com

www.StrutLikeYourMutt.com

www.GlobalPawsForPeace.org

CHAMP
THE HUMAN
WHISPERER

Unleashing the Wisdom of Man's Best Friend

Dr. Harmony

HARMONY Lighthouse PUBLISHING

Sedona, Arizona

Champ The Human Whisperer:
Unleashing the Wisdom of Man's Best Friend

Published by Harmony Lighthouse Publishing
First Edition, 2024
ISBN: 979-8-9915090-0-8

Library of Congress Cataloging-in-Publication Data
Harmony, Dr.
Champ The Human Whisperer: Unleashing the Wisdom of Man's Best Friend /
by Dr. Harmony — 1st ed.

Summary: This book shares the wisdom and lessons of Champ, a Staffordshire Bull Terrier, emphasizing the spiritual bond between humans and dogs and offering 8 timeless tricks for personal transformation.

1. Pets—Psychology, 2. Self-help techniques, 3. Dogs—Behavior, 4. Human-animal relationships, 5. Dogs—Training, 6. Spiritual life.

Library of Congress Control Number (LCCN): 2024919628

Disclaimer: This book is intended for informational and educational purposes only. The content within this book does not constitute medical, psychological, or veterinary advice. Always seek the advice of your physician, mental health professional, or veterinarian with any questions you may have regarding a medical condition, mental health issue, or pet's health. Reliance on any information provided in this book is solely at your own risk.

Printed in the United States of America.

For more information about the author, upcoming books, and events, please visit www.GlobalPawsForPeace.org.

PAWSITIVE PRAISE

"As the curator of Animal Haven, a foster program for animals of all types, I see the struggles of pet owners who love their pets and have to surrender them to someone else's care. Dr. Harmony strikes a chord as she recounts her bond with Champ and their shared life. I was moved to tears more than once by sheer joy and solemn reflection as I took this journey with her in this masterfully crafted and emotionally charged 'tail' of Love and Lessons."

— Seth Byerley, Animal Haven Curator in Sedona, Arizona

"Dr. Harmony's new book was an eye-opening journey into the magical relationship between humans and their pets. I thoroughly enjoyed reading about her adventures with Champ and their synchronicities. Her storytelling ability makes you feel as if you were right there with them, experiencing the joys and lessons together. As a loyal advocate of pit bulls, I was also impressed by how she educated readers about bully breeds. I highly recommend this book. Be prepared for an emotional read—you might not have dry eyes by the end!"

— Anna Dornier, Pitbull Advocate & Sales Systems Architect

"*Champ The Human Whisperer* offers a touching and inspiring perspective on the bond between dogs and humans. Dr. Harmony's storytelling is truly heartfelt, captivating, and creative. A real page-turner!"

— G. Brian Benson, Award-Winning Author, Speaker, and Creative

"Once in a while, a book comes along that not only teaches you valuable life lessons but also tugs at your heartstrings. *Champ The Human Whisperer* is one of them! Dr. Harmony and her beloved Champ take you on an inspiring and emotional journey to awaken your inner champion. So grab a box of tissues and unleash the dog lover in you!"

— Elissa Hope, Best-Selling Author of *Hope From Heaven*

"As Dr. Harmony reflects on the journey of her beloved dog Champ, we experience the true meaning of the joys and trials of being alive. This loving tribute reminds us of the profound, ineffable connection we have with our pets that heals us and walks us home. Reading this book and embodying the lessons from this one-of-a-kind pet is a delicious treat to relish in Champ's honor. A must-read for anyone who cherishes the deep bond with their furry companion."

— Gina Reichert, French Teacher

"Who are our spiritual teachers? In *Champ The Human Whisperer,* Dr. Harmony reveals that some of our most profound teachers are often our pet companions. This heartfelt true story shows how Champ, a beloved pet, offered deep and powerful insights into love, loyalty, and healing. As the author of *Tarot Life Lessons*, Dr. Harmony beautifully intertwines spiritual insights on the soul's journey and interconnectedness. This book stands as a testament to the wisdom, love, and resilience found in our furry friends."

— Julia Gordon-Bramer, Author of *Tarot Life Lessons*

"Wow!!! What an amazing book! *Champ The Human Whisperer* truly captures the essence of an extraordinary dog. I met Champ, and instantly my heart opened and I fell in love! His pure joy, playfulness, and eagerness to connect mirrored the inner work I was doing. Being in his presence and reading about his uninhibited spirit and lack of barriers taught me to open up, be vulnerable, and trust that all is well. Thank you, Champ, for your incredible example and for inspiring us through this excellent book!"

— Kelly Gedeon, Champ's Fan and Supporter

"Dr. Harmony's book is outstanding, offering profound insights into the unshakable bond between her and Champ. Her narrative beautifully illustrates the deep, emotional ties we have with our pets. This book is a must-read for those seeking to understand the true essence of pet companionship."

— Tessa Greenspan, Influential Businesswoman
and Best-Selling Author of
From Outhouse to Penthouse:
Life Lessons on Love, Laughter, and Leadership

For my Soulmate, Champ Avalon
January 28, 2010 - May 10, 2024

You were not just a dog but my best friend, confidant, and greatest teacher. Your boundless love and unwavering loyalty have forever imprinted on my heart. Through every tail wag, every joyful bark, and every gentle nudge, you brought light into my life and taught me the true meaning of unconditional love.

Thank you for choosing me to navigate your mission with you and for all the lessons you taught me. Your presence in my life is a gift I will always cherish. Being with you forever would not have been long enough. To be your voice is an honor beyond words.

I will love you forever with my whole being.

Until we meet again,
Momma

CONTENTS

INTRODUCTION

"I thought I was going to die."

Life had thrown me challenge after challenge, leaving me feeling hopeless and lost. Tough times, heartbreaks, and losses pushed me into a deep, dark place. Every day felt like a struggle in those darkest moments, and I couldn't find my way out. But then came Champ—a bright light in my life—a Staffordshire Bull Terrier and dog guru with a big "Staffie smile." He wasn't just a pet; he became my best friend and guide, helping me rediscover myself and find a new path forward.

Champ's journey is one of love, resilience, and the transformative power of the human-canine bond. As the smallest pup in his litter, he defied the odds, spreading joy and raising awareness about bully breeds. By assisting Champ with his mission through the *100-Day Smile Challenge*—where we aimed to make 100 people smile in 100 days—I discovered a way to overcome my depression. This initiative eventually led to the founding of *Global Paws for Peace,* promoting unity among dogs and humans.

Champ The Human Whisperer explores the remarkable bond between humans and dogs, showing how our canine companions serve as teachers, healers, and guides. Champ's story, from a tiny pup to a wise elder, highlights the profound lessons our dogs can teach us when we genuinely listen to their wisdom. The concept of "The Human Whisperer" lies at the heart of this story—it's about how dogs like Champ connect with us on a deep, spiritual level, offering insights that guide us toward compassion, authenticity, and a fulfilling life. By embracing these teachings, you, too, can find light in the darkest moments, just as Champ helped me do.

Imagine waking up every day feeling lost, struggling to find purpose, and dealing with loneliness, self-doubt, and past hurts. It can be hard to see any light in your life when you feel trapped by your circumstances and unable to move forward.

Now, picture yourself breaking free from that darkness and entering a life filled with love and fulfillment. Through the lessons I learned from Champ, you can begin to cherish the present moment, cultivate deep self-love, and find joy in everyday experiences. These teachings are not just about my journey—they are principles for transforming your life and awakening to the unique purpose your own dog might be revealing to you. Let this message inspire you to see the light and unleash your best self, with your canine companion leading the way.

What You'll Learn

This book is divided into three parts, leading you through Champ's remarkable life and the transformative lessons I learned from him. Each section reflects what you may need to discover within yourself. It is filled with humor, dog language, and Champ's unique messages and offers an engaging and relatable journey.

Part One: Champ's Journey and the Wisdom of Dogs

- **The Science Behind the Bond:** Explore why dogs and humans share such a deep connection, with insights into the psychological and physiological benefits.

- **Waking Up Your Inner Champ:** Discover how Champ's life challenges and triumphs can inspire you to overcome your own obstacles.

- **Living the ABCs of a Champion:** Learn key traits like adaptability, bravery, and courage that can shape your life.

- **Spiritual Connection:** Reflect on the spiritual bond between humans and dogs and how they can guide us.

- **Meet the Mighty Staffy:** Learn about the Staffordshire Bull Terrier's history and resilience.

- **Why Humans Judge:** Challenge and change perceptions about bully breeds by understanding human judgments.

- **Tail-Wagging Legacy:** Continue Champ's mission of spreading positive change.

Part Two: Unleashing Canine Wisdom - 8 Timeless Tricks for Your Best Self

This part is a roadmap to becoming your best self, filled with stories and wisdom from Champ that direct you toward joy, purpose, and love. Each trick offers practical steps to transform your life:

- **Bury Your Bones by Letting Go:** Release the past for growth.

- **Living in Pooch Time Consciousness:** Stay present and enjoy each moment.

- **Bark Out Loud - Speak Your Truth:** Find the courage to express yourself.

- **Love is a Four-Legged Word:** Embrace unconditional love.

- **Sniff It Out - Trust Your Instincts:** Follow your intuition.

- **Become Your Own Best Friend:** Cultivate self-love and compassion.

- **Wag Your Tail and Have Fun Doing It!:** Bring joy and playfulness into your life.

- **Finding Your Paws and Peace Zone:** Balance life's challenges and rewards to find inner peace.

Part Three: Champ's Golden Years - Reflections and Farewell

A look into Champ's later years, his wisdom, and his final journey:

- **Golden Years Reflections:** Insights into the lessons Champ taught in his senior years.

- **Adapting as a Champion:** Lessons on adaptability and perseverance.

- **The Last Adventures:** Heartwarming stories of our final adventures together.

- **A Hero's Farewell:** The emotional journey of saying goodbye and honoring Champ's legacy.

- **Healing from Grief:** Explore the deep bond with pets, how their absence is profoundly felt, and how Champ's lessons can help navigate loss, strengthen memories, and endure love.

With over 30 years in vibrational medicine and a background in chiropractic, my life's work has focused on clearing energetic blockages, aligning spiritual energies, and empowering clients to manifest their highest potential. The profound lessons I learned from my beloved dog, Champ, have shaped my journey as a quantum healer, transformational mentor, best-selling author, and award-winning card deck creator.

Inspired by Champ's mission and my deep passion for dogs, especially bully breeds, I became known as the 'Mother Teresa of Canines.' This devotion led to the founding of *Global Paws for Peace,* a non-profit organization that fosters unity among all breeds and humans. At *Global Paws for Peace,* we strive to create a world where compassion, understanding, and acceptance transcend boundaries. Our work focuses on empowering humans with knowledge, empathy, and love, enriching the lives of our beloved dogs.

This handbook is more than just a collection of dog stories; it's a heartfelt manual to living a meaningful, joyful, and fulfilling life. With Champ's guidance, you'll find the strength to break free from past hurts and self-doubt, building a life filled with happiness, meaning, and love. *Champ The Human Whisperer* is a blueprint for a fulfilling life for anyone ready to follow his lead.

Champ's love taught me to overcome challenges, wake up my inner champion, and live consciously. You'll learn to tap into the wisdom of your best canine friend, just as I did with Champ, to face life's obstacles and live your best life, one *paw* step at a time.

As we begin this journey, open your heart and mind to Champ's lessons. We'll explore the deep connection between humans and dogs, starting with the history of the canine-human bond and how Champ's legacy has left an indelible mark on the world.

So, grab a cozy spot—maybe with your furry friend by your side—and get ready for a tail-wagging adventure. We'll start with the mysteries of the ancient bond between humans and dogs, setting the stage to unleash the wisdom of man's best friend and help you stop chasing your tail and start truly living.

Ready to fetch some wisdom?
Let's get started!

MESSAGE FROM CHAMP: WISDOM FROM THE HEART

Hey there, Pawsome Reader!

I'm *Champ Avalon,* the Staffordshire Bull Terrier with the legendary "Staffie smile" that makes tails wag worldwide. Momma says my grin is like a ray of sunshine, spreading joy wherever I go, and I agree! My journey started with *ruff* challenges. They said I'd never measure up to my champion bloodline, but here I am, proving them wrong daily!

I may have been pint-sized, but now that I've crossed the rainbow bridge, my spirit is as big as the sky! With Momma keeping my message alive, I've fetched some life lessons that'll make your heart sing, and I can't wait to share them in this *barktastic* book.

I'm not just any dog—I'm an ambassador for my fellow bully breeds on a mission to unleash their full *pawtential.* Together with Momma, we're on a *pawsitive* quest to educate and inspire others to see past the stereotypes and end breed-specific legislation (BSL).

But it doesn't stop there. I'm here to help you dig deep, uncover hidden strengths, and embrace what makes you uniquely powerful. If you're ready to live your best life, open your heart and trust your instincts. I'm here to guide you every step of the way!

Living in *pooch-time consciousness (PTC)* is a howl! It's about finding freedom, joy, and that warm fuzzy feeling in your heart. Being a champion isn't just about winning—it's about finding love, peace, and happiness within yourself.

So, if you're eager to start, keep reading. I'll show you how to chase your dreams, fetch enjoyment, and make this adventure with Momma and me your best one yet.

Ready?

Let's get our paws a little dirty! 🐾

Champ Avalon

PART ONE

CHAMP'S JOURNEY AND THE WISDOM OF DOGS

CHAPTER 01

MAN'S BEST FRIEND: UNLEASHING THE BOND BETWEEN HUMANS AND DOGS

Ever wonder why dogs are called "Man's Best Friend"? It's not because they can fetch a ball or wag their tails like pros; it's because they embody loyalty, companionship, and an unconditional love that makes our own hearts wag with joy. From the dawn of time to today's cozy dog beds, the bond between humans and dogs has only grown stronger, transforming both species in ways we can't begin to sniff out.

Picture a world without dogs. No tail-wagging greetings, no joyful barks echoing through the park, no warm, furry bodies curling up next to us after a long day. *It's a ruff thought, isn't it?* Dogs have been our sidekicks for thousands of years, evolving alongside us, adapting to our needs, and bringing endless joy.

In this chapter, we'll dig into the magic of this unique connection, uncovering why dogs are our ultimate partners in life.

We'll trot through history, tracing our bond back to ancient times when dogs were more than just pets—they were hunters, guardians, and even spiritual guides. From loyal protectors to skilled bloodhounds and therapy fluffballs to our best furry friends, dogs have worn many collars throughout history. Along the way, we'll explore the science behind this bond, revealing the emotional and psychological connections that make our relationship with dogs so special.

Let's celebrate the enduring friendship between humans and their canine companions through heartwarming 'tails' of heroism and unwavering service. Grab a leash, a treat, and maybe a tissue or two.

From Howling Wolves to Happy Woofs: The Historical Origins of Man's Best Friend

The bond between humans and dogs is one of history's oldest and most enduring relationships. This connection began when wild wolves decided to cozy up to our ancient ancestors, likely around 20,000 to 40,000 years ago during the Stone Age.

Early humans and wolves roamed the same environments, pursuing the same game. Over time, a mutually beneficial relationship blossomed. With their sharp senses and hunting prowess, wolves became valuable partners for tracking and hunting. Early humans provided food and protection in return, creating a win-win situation. Imagine the first time a wolf thought, *Hey, these two-legged creatures have great taste in leftovers!*

Generations of wolves started hanging around human camps, enjoying the perks of easy meals and warmth. Those that were friendlier and less aggressive began to integrate into human society. These proto-dogs evolved physically and behaviorally to better fit their new roles. Over thousands of years, selective breeding further refined these early dogs, enhancing traits that made them perfect companions and helpers.

I can see those ancient wolf dogs lounging by the fire, pondering, *I've got a good gig here—free food, and all I have to do is wag my tail and look cute!* Understanding this ancient bond helps us appreciate our deep connection with dogs today.

Let's dive into the many roles dogs have fulfilled throughout history, showcasing their invaluable contributions as loyal companions, protectors, and more. Evolving from their wild wolf ancestors to

4

becoming our closest friends, dogs have consistently demonstrated why they hold such a special place in our lives.

The Ever-Changing Roles of Man's Best Friend

Throughout history, dogs have ingrained their place as invaluable partners to humans. Their roles have evolved, adapting to the needs and cultures of the times. Here are just a few examples of the roles dogs have played in companionship with humans:

- **Hunting Buddies:** One of dogs' earliest roles was assisting in hunting. Their superior sense of smell, speed, and endurance made them excellent partners in tracking and capturing prey. Dogs could locate game that humans might have missed, leading to more successful hunts and providing a vital food source for primitive communities. Imagine a dog reflecting, *If I find this deer, maybe I'll get an extra bone tonight!*

- **Herding Heroes:** As human societies transitioned from nomadic hunting and gathering to settled agricultural lifestyles, dogs adapted to new roles. Herding dogs became indispensable in managing livestock, protecting them from predators and guiding them to grazing areas. Breeds like Border Collies and Australian Shepherds are prime examples of dogs specifically bred for their herding abilities. Picture a Border Collie rounding up sheep, probably wondering, *Why am I not getting a raise for this? (he-he)*

- **Furry Protectors:** Historically, guard dogs have been trained to defend homes and livestock from intruders and predators. Their loyalty and naturally protective instincts made them guardians, providing security in uncertain times. It's like having a furry security system that gets paid in belly rubs.

- **Service Superstars:** Dogs have been employed in various service roles, from pulling sleds in Arctic regions to acting as sentinels in wartime. More recently, they have been trained as

5

police and military dogs, search-and-rescue animals, and service dogs for individuals with disabilities. Their intelligence, trainability, and keen senses make them ideal for these critical tasks. When Champ wore his service vest, he thought, *Just another day at the office, helping my Momma and being pawesome!*

Dogs have seamlessly adapted to our ever-changing human world, showcasing their incredible versatility and steadfast loyalty. Their roles have morphed from hunters and herders to beloved pets. Yet, their unwavering commitment to us remains a constant. Champ always waited by the door, ready to greet me with a wagging tail, whether I was gone for five minutes or five hours.

Their ability to adapt while staying devoted makes them exceptional partners in our journey through life. Dogs have earned their place as family members who stand by us through thick and thin, embodying the true spirit of "Man's Best Friend."

The Pawsome Perks of Our Canine Companions

Dogs' unwavering loyalty, deep empathy, steadfast friendship, and unconditional love profoundly impact our lives. Let's dig into what makes these traits so unique and why we connect with our furry friends on such a deep, heartfelt level, with a dash of dog humor to keep things light and fun.

Fur-tastic Loyalty

Countless stories and legends immortalize dogs' unwavering loyalty. This extraordinary bond showcases how deeply our canine friends commit to us.

- *Faithful Sidekicks:* Dogs stick by our sides through thick and thin, offering steadfast commitment. Think of them as your furry bodyguards who never take a day off.

- *A Tail of Devotion:* One famous story is that of Hachiko, an Akita dog from Japan. Every day, Hachiko waited at the Shibuya train station for his owner, even after his owner passed away. Hachiko continued this daily ritual for nearly ten years until his own death, becoming a symbol of unwavering loyalty and devotion. *He was likely thinking, I'm here every day—where's my best friend?*

Sniffing Out Empathy

Dogs can sense and respond to human emotions, making them invaluable companions during distress.

- *Emotional Sensitivity:* Dogs pick up on subtle changes in our moods and behaviors. They often respond with comforting actions, such as resting their head on our lap or gently nudging us, offering silent support. It's like having a furry therapist who works for treats.

- *Champ's Magic Touch:* Champ had an uncanny ability to sense when I was feeling down. During moments of sadness, he would sit close to me, his presence providing a soothing and calming effect. *I know Champ believed, Momma is sad; I must give her snuggles.*

Pawsome Companionship

Dogs provide unmatched friendship. They offer presence and comfort that can alleviate loneliness and isolation.

- *Constant Companions:* Dogs are always there for us, ready to share our joys and sorrows. Their playful antics and affectionate behavior can brighten even the darkest days. They're like the ultimate roommates who never leave dishes in the sink.

- *Winter Warriors:* During the winter of my battle with COVID-19, Champ's companionship was a lifeline. Despite the harsh weather, taking him out for daily walks, even during a blizzard, was never a burden. His unwavering love brought a sense of normalcy and comfort during a challenging time. *Champ was always ready to go out, Snow? No problem. Let's go!*

Unconditional Love Woofs

Dogs' most cherished quality is their capacity for unconditional love. They love us without judgment or conditions.

- *Non-Judgmental Affection:* Dogs do not care about our flaws or mistakes. They love us for who we are, providing a safe space to be our true selves. It's like having a fan club that cheers for you no matter what.

- *Champ's Unwavering Love:* Champ was my constant after many failed relationships. He was the one who never left, always there for me no matter what. His presence taught me that true love doesn't waver with circumstances; it remains steadfast. In return, I committed to always being there for him, no matter what challenges came our way. *Champ's Motto was, I'll love you forever, treats or no treats.*

Understanding these *timeless traits* helps us truly appreciate the deep bond we share with our four-legged friends, which enriches our lives in countless ways. Picture your furry buddy's excitement when you walk through the door—they don't care if you had a bad day or made mistakes.

That's what Champ did for me. Thanks to him, I've learned to live more in the moment and embrace life's simple pleasures.

Now, let's dig into the science behind this incredible bond. *What is it about dogs that allows them to connect with us so deeply and provide such profound companionship?* Let's sniff out the facts and explore the unique qualities that make our relationship with dogs so memorable.

The Nose Knows: The Science Behind the Bond

The bond between humans and dogs is one of nature's most extraordinary relationships. Researchers have spent years figuring out what lies behind this exceptional connection.

Sniffing Out the Research

Scientists have dug deep to understand the dynamics of the human-canine bond. From evolution to brain chemistry, they've uncovered some unique insights:

- **Evolutionary Tail-Wagging:** Dogs and humans have evolved together, forming a unique partnership that benefits both species. This co-evolution has made dogs incredibly attuned to our emotions and behaviors.

- **Mind-Reading Mutts:** Studies show dogs can understand human gestures, respond to emotions, and even follow our gaze. They know precisely what is about to happen without words. *It's like they're thinking, Oh, that look means it's bath time!* And we have all seen the priceless looks on their faces when they don't want to take a bath.

- **Brainy Barkers:** Advances in brain imaging have allowed scientists to see what happens in the brains of dogs and humans during interactions. Both species experience *pawsitive* emotions.

Biological and Psychological Pawsitivity

Several scientific factors shape the strong bond between humans and dogs. Let's review a couple of the top reasons we experience biological and physiological connections with our dogs:

- **Oxytocin Overload:** Known as the "love hormone," oxytocin is released during interactions like petting and playing. This hormone stimulates affection and bonding. Looking into each other's eyes releases oxytocin and strengthens the bond. Studies show that dogs and humans experience mutual joy during these moments. I presume dogs think, *This eye contact is like magic!*

- **Emotional Pawsitivity:** Emotional transference happens when one individual's emotions trigger similar feelings in another. Dogs can mirror human emotions, creating a shared experience.

9

Research shows dogs are likely to comfort their owners who are feeling down.

From oxytocin boosts to emotional mirroring, dogs and humans share a tie that enriches our lives in countless ways. So, the next time you gaze into your dog's eyes, remember—there's a lot of science (and a lot of love) behind that wagging tail!

The Healing Power of Canine Companionship: Pawsitive Medicine

Dogs are like furry superheroes whose power comes from wagging tails that have healing energy! They offer emotional support and comfort that can turn even the gloomiest day into a joyful adventure. Let's fetch some insights into how these four-legged therapists work their magic.

Dogs have an incredible knack for sensing human emotions. They can detect when we're feeling down, anxious, or stressed. Their empathetic nature makes them perfect emotional support animals. Champ wasn't just a furry friend—he was my emotional anchor during tough times.

Paws on Duty: The Therapeutic Roles of Dogs

Dogs wear many hats (and sometimes cute little vests) in their roles as healers. Let's break down these therapeutic roles:

Super Service Dogs

These canine heroes assist individuals with disabilities, performing tasks like guiding the visually impaired, alerting the hearing impaired, and helping with mobility. They're like superhero sidekicks, always ready to lend a paw.

Illustration: Picture a guide dog leading its owner through a busy street, carefully navigating around obstacles, thinking, *Stick with me, human. I've got your back!*

Therapy Dogs: Professional Cuddlers

Therapy dogs spread joy and comfort in hospitals, nursing homes, and schools. They're like professional cuddlers on a mission to make everyone smile.

> *Illustration:* Envision a therapy dog visiting a hospital, making rounds, and bringing smiles to patients' faces. The dog probably thinks, *My job is to spread happiness—and I nailed it!*

Emotional Support Animals: Furry Therapists

These dogs provide comfort and alleviate symptoms of emotional or psychological conditions. They don't need specialized training but offer stability and comfort during challenging times. Champ's certification as an emotional support dog was a testament to his vital role in my healing journey.

> *Illustration:* Whenever Champ sensed my stress, he would instantly curl up beside me as if to say, *Don't worry, Momma. I'm here for you.*

A Dose of Fur-tastic Therapy

Research has shown that interactions with dogs can lead to significant health benefits. Here are a few ways they support our well-being:

- **Lower Stress Levels:** Petting a dog can lower cortisol levels (the stress hormone) and increase oxytocin (the bonding hormone), promoting relaxation and happiness.

- **Heart Health:** Dog owners often have lower blood pressure and cholesterol levels, thanks to the regular exercise and stress relief that come with dog ownership.

- **Mental Well-being:** Dogs help reduce symptoms of depression and anxiety by providing companionship and a sense of *pawpose.*

Dogs are not just pets but healers with *paws* and wagging tails. Whether they're guiding us through life's obstacles, cuddling us through tough times, or simply making us laugh with their antics, dogs genuinely have a healing touch that's hard to beat.

The Profound Wisdom of Dogs: Life Lessons from Our Canine Companions

Dogs possess an extraordinary ability to touch our lives in profound ways that transcend mere companionship. They are not just pets and healers but teachers who help us navigate life's complexities. Through their loyalty, limitless love, and intuitive understanding, dogs like Champ offer invaluable lessons that enrich our lives and promote personal growth. Let's fetch some insights into how these four-legged sages impart their wisdom.

Pawsome Intuitive Guides

Dogs have a knack for sensing our emotions and giving us exactly what we need, whether it's a cuddle, a friend, or just being there. They often understand us better than we know ourselves. Their empathy and intuition make them exceptional guides through life's ups and downs.

- **Emotional Sensitivity:** Dogs can sense subtle changes in our emotions. They know when we're sad, stressed, or anxious and often respond with comforting actions like laying their heads on our laps or simply staying close by. It's like having a furry therapist who doesn't charge by the hour!

- **Instinctive Support:** When life gets overwhelming, dogs remind us to take a break and enjoy the simple pleasures. Their playful antics and joyous spirit can bring a smile to our faces. Over the years, Champ taught me to take what I called "bubby breaks." I Intentionally paused multiple times throughout the day to give Champ attention while he brought me back into the present moment.

- **Pure Instincts:** Dogs are guided by pure instincts, not cluttered with the human monkey mind. Their actions are driven by a natural understanding and connection to the world around them.

This purity of instinct allows them to respond to situations with clarity and honesty, making them amazing role models for living authentically. Embracing this concept can help us trust our own instincts more and live more naturally and freely.

Life Lessons from Our Canine Companions

Champ was my greatest teacher, helping me through the toughest times. His presence gave me comfort and strength, showing me resilience and unconditional love. Here are some timeless lessons we can learn from our dogs:

Live in the Moment

Dogs are masters at living in the present. They don't dwell on the past or worry about the future. Champ taught me to embrace each moment fully and find joy in the simple things—like a good belly rub or a romp in the park. In a forthcoming chapter, we'll dive into living in the present moment in *Champ's Trick #2, Living in Pooch Time Consciousness,* he'll show us how to be more conscious and live consciously.

Champ's Philosophy: Life's too short—chase the squirrel and enjoy every moment!

Unconditional Love and Loyalty:

Dogs don't care about our flaws or mistakes; they accept us for who we are. Champ's unwavering loyalty showed me the true meaning of unconditional love.

Champ's Motto: My job is to spread happiness—mission accomplished! Every day's a tail-wagging adventure with you!

Resilience in Adversity:

Dogs face challenges with a *pawsitive* attitude and a wagging tail. Whether it's a trip to the vet or adapting to new surroundings, they demonstrate remarkable stability. Champ's fearlessness in the face of adversity inspired me to stay strong and hopeful.

Champ's Wisdom: When life gets tough, wag harder!

The Joy of Simplicity:

Dogs find happiness in the simplest things—a game of fetch, a cozy nap, or a tasty treat. They remind us that joy doesn't have to be complicated. Champ's enthusiasm for everyday activities taught me to appreciate the little things.

Champ's Insight: Every day is a new adventure—let's make the most of it!

Champ's Legacy as a Teacher and Healer

For over 14 years, Champ was more than just a friend; he was (and still is) my most incredible mentor and healer. After enduring a series of life-altering events and battling COVID-19, I was diagnosed with Post-Traumatic Stress Syndrome (PTSD). The psychological toll was immense, and Champ's role became even more crucial during this challenging time.

Recognizing his profound impact on my emotional well-being, I had Champ certified as an emotional support dog. His presence provided a sense of security and stability, helping me navigate the complexities of PTSD and aiding in my recovery. Champ's constant companionship was like a beacon of light, guiding me through the darkest periods. His attitude seemed to say, *We've got this, Momma. One paw at a time!*

Champ's intuitive understanding of my emotional state and unwavering love helped me regain a sense of routine and hope. Through his presence, I discovered the profound emotional support dogs offer and the unique healing power of the human-canine bond. He taught me many things, but at the top of the list are resilience, patience, and the power of unconditional love. *His advice? Stay strong, and don't forget the treats!*

We learn from dogs to embrace affection, happiness, and strength. Their profound wisdom can guide us to live more fulfilling lives filled with compassion. Champ's legacy continues to inspire me to be my best self and see the world through a dog's eyes—full of wonder and limitless affection.

The lessons Champ imparted gave birth to this book, ensuring that his wisdom and love continue to touch lives even after his passing. His mission of spreading happiness, love, and acceptance lives on through these pages, encouraging others to embrace his embodied principles. Champ's journey was not just about friendship but about fulfilling a *pawpose* and leaving a legacy of love.

The Unbreakable Bond Between Humans and Dogs

As we wrap up this chapter, it's time to reflect on our incredible journey through the enduring bond between humans and dogs. From wolves by ancient campfires to the multifaceted roles our furry friends play today, it's clear that dogs are more than pets—they are loyal companions, intuitive healers, and steadfast friends.

History and science show us how these remarkable animals have been our hunting partners, herding helpers, protectors, and emotional supporters. They've adapted to our changing world with versatility and unwavering commitment.

The essence of the human-canine bond lies in the wisdom and lessons our dogs teach us. They instill courage and *pawseverance* and are some of our best mentors.

Having explored the bond between humans and dogs, we now dive into Champ's journey. His life exemplifies happiness, compassion, and unity.

Let's trot on over to the next chapter, *Champ's Lessons and Legacy: Waking Up Your Inner Champ* and uncover the timeless teachings Champ has left us. Get ready to *emBARK* on a journey of self-discovery.

CHAPTER 02

CHAMP'S LESSON'S
AND LEGACY:
WAKING UP YOUR
INNER CHAMP

In the grand 'tail' of life, some souls leave paw prints on our hearts that last forever. None have impacted me more than Champ, my steadfast Staffordshire Bull Terrier. His legacy transcends time and space, touching lives with his eternal spirit.

Champ's journey is one of triumph, inspiring us to find our inner Champ and reach our full *pawtential*. His life teaches us essential lessons on overcoming adversity, embracing change, and building inner resilience.

In this chapter, we'll explore the invaluable lessons from Champ's extraordinary life. Through his profound wisdom, Champ shows us how to truly know ourselves and awaken our spirits. His gifts are a guiding light, navigating us through the labyrinth of human experiences with strength and courage.

As we journey through his unforgettable expedition, Champ reminds us that greatness lies within each of us, just waiting to be unleashed. Digging deeper into his 'tail,' we discover the powerful transformation that unwavering determination and freedom can bring—waking up a power that resides within us all, ready to be set free.

The Pawsome Beginning of Champ's Journey

Born under miraculous circumstances, Champ arrived as the smallest pup in his litter. He defied the odds and set out on a mission to touch the hearts of everyone he met.

Champ's entry into my life was no coincidence—it was the result of careful planning, thoughtful consideration, and a deep yearning for a canine companion. I had always been drawn to the idea of having a dog with a strong presence and unwavering spirit. My search for the ideal dog took me through various breeds, eventually stumbling onto the Staffordshire Bull Terrier.

My quest led me to Emily, a passionate breeder in Florida whose love for her dogs was evident in every detail of her work. Emily's commitment to breeding healthy, well-tempered dogs aligned perfectly with my desire for a loving and spirited companion.

In a twist of fate, Emily's unique breeding philosophy—limiting her litter deposits to a select few—meant that the slots for the litter were already filled when I reached out. I was placed on a waiting list, eagerly anticipating news of any available puppies. As fate would have it, Champ entered the world as the runt, sparking doubts about his ability to meet breed standards. Yet, he defied expectations and grew into a champion in every sense of the word.

To ensure Champ found the perfect home, Emily intended to list him as a pet rather than a show dog. Recognizing Champ's exceptional qualities, she reached out to me, asking if I would accept him as a pet. Nonetheless, Emily knew Champ possessed one of the finest crowns she had ever seen. Emily questioned that she might miss out on Champ's *pawtential* to be one of her best show dogs.

Though Emily considered keeping Champ, she knew his future lay elsewhere. She sought a loving home, allowing Champ and me to fulfill our fate—a destiny I know was far greater than any competition could define.

Emily witnessed his miraculous arrival. At first, she couldn't believe her eyes. *"Is this a pup?"* Emily wondered, her mind racing with disbelief. But then, as if guided by instinct, she sprang into action, nurturing him with tender care and blowing air into his tiny lungs. With that first gasp for breath, Champ's journey began.

Born barely the size of a thumb, Champ entered the world as a big spirit in a little body. He knew he had a mission to fulfill—a message to spread. I knew in my heart he was meant to be part of my life. I eagerly awaited when I could bring him home and shower him with love and affection.

His early days were spent in an incubator, surrounded by rabbits. Their warmth and companionship shaped his very being. I used to tell him he had bunny ears because they felt like velvet when I rubbed them. Emily gave him special treatment, devoting extra time to ensure his strength and well-being. While his siblings rested in their kennel, Champ basked in the warmth of Emily's room, watching over her daughter as she played video games.

Nurtured with special attention, Champ flourished with each passing day. His distinctive traits and endless vitality distinguished him from his siblings. Emily ensured that Champ received additional care and affection, granting him two special hours each day with his birth momma—a time reserved solely for him.

When I finally arrived to pick Champ up, a remarkable moment unfolded. As soon as he saw me, Champ darted toward the gate where we would be leaving. I felt a profound connection instantly, and his voice echoed within me, whispering, *"Where have you been? I have been waiting on you."* It was as though Champ and I were bound by an unseen thread, our destinies intertwined in a way that transcended mere chance.

This profound encounter marked the beginning of our extraordinary journey together. I realized that Champ was not just a dog; he was my *Soul Companion and Human Whisperer.* Together, we navigated a path of deep connection and understanding, leading each other to new levels of fulfillment.

Through every challenge and triumph, our bond only grew stronger—a testament to the power of love and the mysterious workings of fate. Champ and I were not just companions; we shared an extraordinary partnership, driven by a mutual sense of *pawpose* and an unbreakable connection.

Champ's Journey: A 'Tail' of Resilience and Transformation

Champ's journey is a powerful story of facing challenges with courage and embracing transformation. From the moment he was born, Champ defied the odds. Despite his small size, his spirit was unbreakable, showing that true strength comes from within. His resilience teaches us that no obstacle is insurmountable when met with an open heart and determined spirit.

Champ's life was about more than overcoming adversity; it was about evolving into something greater. His transformation from a tiny pup to a beacon of hope and love illustrates that we are defined not by our circumstances but by how we respond to them.

Witnessing Champ's growth inspired me to confront my own challenges with the same courage and grace. Transformation isn't just about change; it's about becoming our best selves. Champ's example shows us that embracing change leads to personal growth and empowerment.

Life is full of changes, and how we navigate them shapes our experiences. Champ's wagging tail and joyful spirit were constant reminders that we can tackle any challenge and emerge stronger with the right mindset. So, grab your leash of determination, and let Champ's wisdom guide you on your own journey of growth and resilience.

Waking Up Your Inner Champ

As we become more aware, we connect with our spiritual side and uncover deeper truths. Like Champ, who always seemed calm and wise, we can tap into our inner wisdom. Letting go of past hurts and negative thoughts clears the way for inner peace and freedom.

Life's challenges can sometimes feel like stepping in dog poo—getting stuck in the same mess over and over. Letting go means cleaning up past mistakes and finding balance. As we grow, we reach new levels of awareness and sniff out our true *pawpose.*

I've worked with many clients who feel stuck in old habits that keep them from moving forward. Together, we work on shedding those negative layers and embracing truth and inspiration. It's like putting lights on a Christmas tree—each step forward makes our inner light shine brighter for everyone to see.

Awakening your inner Champ means knowing yourself, embracing your spirit, and recognizing your strengths. It involves accepting yourself, including your mistakes, and allowing good things into your life. By listening to your inner voice and aligning with your destiny, you open up to life's magic. Life has few guarantees, but by following Champ's wisdom, you'll find yourself transformed by the end of this journey.

Here are a few *pawsitive* tricks to wake up your inner Champ:

Bounce Back Like a Champ

- *Champ's Journey:* We all face tough times, just like Champ did. How we respond to these challenges really matters. When we bounce back from difficulties, we can learn, grow, and become stronger.

- *Paw-suit:* See challenges as opportunities to grow. Practice mindfulness and consider how you can be more resilient. Accept that change is part of life and focus on adapting *pawsitively.*

Unleash Your True Pawtential

- *Champ's Story:* Champ started small but grew to embody the qualities of a show dog, with strength, power, and poise. We all have hidden talents and strengths waiting to be discovered. Encouraging change helps you tap into your true *pawtential* and develop those qualities.

- *Paw-suit:* Spend time figuring out what you're good at and what you love. Set goals that match your values and dreams. Believe in your ability to learn and succeed.

Find Your Inner Champ

- *Champ's Legacy:* We all have an inner Champ, our best self. This part of us is courageous, confident, and authentic. By finding our inner champion, we can overcome obstacles and achieve our dreams.

- *Paw-suit:* Get to know yourself through meditation, journaling, or talking to someone. Challenge negative thoughts that hold you back. Be kind to yourself and take care of your inner Champ.

Take Inspired Action

- *Champ's Reminder:* To make changes, we need to take action. Knowing our *pawtential* is not enough; we must do something about it. We can create meaningful change by aligning our thoughts, intentions, and actions.

- *Paw-suit:* Set clear objectives that fit your vision for the future. Break big goals into smaller steps and make a plan. Take regular, intentional steps toward your goals and celebrate your progress. Surround yourself with supportive people who inspire you.

By being consistent, discovering our *pawtential,* and unleashing our inner Champ, we can start a journey of self-discovery and personal growth. Committing to our goals allows us to create a *pawposeful* and meaningful life through intentional action.

Unleashing Your Inner Champ: A Journey of Self-Discovery and Paws-formation

EmBARKING on the journey to find your inner Champ means leaving behind life's messes and stepping into the sunny spot of self-awareness, where you discover your true pawtential.

Imagine shifting from chasing your tail to finding your true *pawpose.* It's like feeling more *pawsitive,* creative, and connected to something bigger. To get there, it's time to let go of old habits and negative experiences— think of it as cleaning out your doghouse, tossing what no longer serves you.

Connecting with your higher self means embracing who you truly are. This connection helps you fulfill your life's *pawpose* and find real happiness. The journey of self-discovery and transformation is ongoing. As you grow, you become more attuned to who you're becoming, burying old bones, and welcoming new aspects of yourself.

Here are a few practices to unleash your inner Champ:

Shed the Old Fur

- *Let Go of Old Habits:* Like a dog shedding its old fur, let go of habits and experiences that no longer serve you.

- *Paw-suit:* Identify habits and thoughts that hold you back. Create a plan to replace them with healthier, more empowering practices.

Sniff Out Your True Pawtential

- *Discover Your Strengths:* Dogs have an incredible sense of smell, and you can develop an incredible sense of self. Find your hidden talents and strengths waiting to be discovered.

- *Paw-suit:* Take time to reflect on your passions and skills. Set goals that align with your true *pawtential* and confidently work towards them.

Wag with Pawpose

- *Embrace Your Journey:* Just like a dog wags its tail with joy, embrace your journey of self-discovery with enthusiasm. Every step forward is a step towards your best self.

- *Paw-suit:* Celebrate your progress, no matter how small. Keep a journal to track your journey and recognize each milestone along the way.

Bark Up the Right Tree

- *Make Intentional Choices:* Dogs instinctively know which tree to bark up. Similarly, make intentional choices that align with your goals and values.

- *Paw-suit:* Evaluate your decisions carefully. Choose actions that support your growth and align with your authentic self. *Unleashing your inner Champ* is about recognizing your worth, letting go of the past, and stepping into your true *pawtential.* It's a journey that leads to greater self-awareness, *pawsitivity,* and a deeper connection with the world around you. So, wag your tail, sniff out your opportunities, and fetch your dreams with the spirit of Champ guiding you every step of the way.

Embracing the Lessons of Champ's Journey

Champ's journey shows us how to wake up our inner giant and live our best lives. His victories and struggles remind us to be strong and overcome challenges. By learning these lessons, you can awaken your inner Champ and tackle life's obstacles with confidence and style.

Take a moment to honor your furry friend's valuable lessons. Their spirit guides you to be your best self, showing you the power of love and bravery.

Remember, every wag of the tail and joyful bark brings you closer to boundless joy and fulfillment. Welcome to the next chapter of your adventure, where the real fun and rewards begin!

Now, let's trot on over and *embrace the ABCs of living like a Champ.* Your journey to a richer, more fulfilling life has just begun, and Champ and I are here to cheer you on every step of the way.

CHAPTER 03

WAGGING THROUGH THE ABCS OF LIVING THE LIFE OF A CHAMP

What if I told you that the key to a joyful, pawposeful life lies in the simple wisdom of a dog? From the moment Champ trotted into my world, he began sharing extraordinary lessons. These insights are distilled into the ABCs of living like a true Champ. They've guided me through life's puddles and belly rubs, teaching me to grow and change with a wagging tail.

Champ's name perfectly captured his spirit and qualities. Being a Champ is more than just earning a title; it's about embodying strength, courage, and a heart ready for every new adventure. Champ lived these traits, inspiring everyone around him to rise above challenges and discover their own inner strength.

As I reflect on my journey with Champ, I see how his wisdom has shaped my life. From struggles to joy-filled moments, Champ's guidance has been a bright, wagging tail leading me toward greater self-awareness and personal growth. Now, as we dive into the ABCs together, I invite you to open your heart to these timeless teachings and embrace their transformative power.

In this chapter, we'll explore these guiding principles, with each letter of the ABCs representing a core aspect of Champ's teachings. We'll uncover how these simple yet profound lessons can help us unleash our true *pawtential* and live our best lives.

Let's fetch some wisdom and have a barking good time!

The Origin of Champ's Name: Unleashing Greatness

Fourteen years ago, when I named my dog "Champp Avalon," I had no idea of the more profound significance behind the name. The AKC wouldn't allow "Champ" on his birth certificate, but I was determined to honor his destined greatness. So, I added an extra "p" and named him "Champp." Little did I know, this name choice came from a place deeper than conscious thought.

To me, a "Champp" is an ordinary being doing extraordinary things. From the beginning, I knew Champ was destined for greatness. He wasn't just a dog but a beacon of hope and resilience. According to the dictionary, a champion is a winner who excels and enjoys victories. This *pawfectly* encapsulates Champ's spirit and his remarkable impact on my life.

The name "Avalon" carries significant meaning in Celtic legend. Avalon is an island represented as an earthly paradise where King Arthur and other heroes were carried at death. It signifies bringing heaven to earth, a concept that resonated deeply with me during a transformative visit to the Isle of Avalon in England. Over time, I realized that naming him *Champp Avalon* was no coincidence. It reflected our soul connection and his noble heritage. No wonder he always acted so royal, and I affectionately called him *Sir Avalon* since he was a puppy.

During a pivotal moment in my life, I experienced a significant change and awakened the Champ within me. After my divorce and needing to change my previous name, I adopted Champ's last name. My son-in-law's reaction was priceless: *"You're taking your dog's last name?"* To which I responded, *"Yes."* It symbolized more than just a name change. It represented a profound connection to my roots and a previous soul connection with Champ in Avalon. It was a step towards embracing my true identity and honoring the bond Champ and I share.

Champ's name is more than just a label; it's a testament to his extraordinary spirit and transformative impact on my life and the world. It signifies resilience, triumph, and the journey of bringing a little bit of heaven to earth through our shared experiences.

Understanding Champ's name and heritage provides a deeper insight into our remarkable connection. As we move forward, we'll explore how this bond has paved the way for embracing the ABCs of living the life of a true Champ. We can all learn to unleash our true *pawtential* and live our best lives through Champ's lessons and timeless tricks.

Sniffing Out the ABCs of Living the Life of a Champ

One ordinary day, while driving down the road, I experienced a moment of clarity that forever changed how I understood Champ's teachings. Reflecting on the power of the 8 tricks I'll share in part two of this book, I felt deep gratitude for the lessons Champ had imparted. Little did I know this day would reveal yet another layer of his wisdom.

As I drove, I suddenly heard Champ's voice in my head, loud and clear: *"Champ taught Momma her ABCs."* The message was so powerful that I had to pull over. I grabbed my notebook and pen, and the words flowed effortlessly, as if guided by a force beyond my understanding. Champ's ABCs came to life before my eyes, each letter representing a guiding principle for living a virtuous life.

Interestingly, right after this revelation, a friend contacted me to ask if I was planning to attend a cruise where Dr. Wayne Dyer would be teaching the Beatitudes. The Beatitudes, part of the Sermon on the Mount, have always held a special place in my heart. Wayne's teachings on the Beatitudes offer profound insights into the attitudes and behaviors that lead to a blessed and fulfilling life. They align perfectly with the message I had just received from Champ. Receiving Champ's *Be-Attitudes* felt like more than a coincidence; it was a divine alignment, a confirmation that Champ's ABCs were ancient wisdom to living a life of true spiritual fulfillment.

Em"BARK"ing on the ABCs of Living the Life of a Champ

Living like a Champ means embracing love, inner peace, and joy. Champ's ABCs are like modern-day guideposts, each one highlighting a key part of his teachings. From awareness to compassion, these principles help us unlock our true *pawtential* and fully enjoy life.

Champ's wisdom has shown me that even when life throws us a curveball, we have the strength to overcome and transform. The ABCs include awareness, which helps us see our strengths and weaknesses, and acceptance, which encourages us to embrace all parts of ourselves. Being grateful brings grace into our lives, and compassion opens our hearts to unconditional love. These qualities create a foundation for a meaningful and joyful life.

As we sniff out the ABCs of *living like a Champ,* we'll explore each principle in detail and see how they can transform our lives. By embracing these ideas, we can face life's challenges with a wagging tail and an open heart, ready to fetch the best out of every situation.

Ready for a tail-wagging adventure? Onward!

Pawsome Breakdown: The ABCs of Living Like a Champ

Each letter of the ABCs represents a key lesson from Champ, guiding us toward a fulfilled life. Here's what each letter stands for and how you can practice it's meaning:

A's: Attitudes of Empowerment

Introducing the A's of living the life of a Champ! These principles are the pillars of Champ's wisdom. Explore how practicing these mindsets can transform your life.

- *Awareness is Pawsome:* Awareness of your thoughts, emotions, and actions is the first step to transformation.
- *Accept All That Is:* Embrace the present moment and accept things as they are, just like a pup enjoying a sunny spot.
- *Ask for a Helping Paw:* Don't hesitate to seek help when needed.
- *Appreciation Brings Grace:* Cultivating gratitude attracts *pawsitive* energy and blessings.
- *Action Unleashes Your Dreams:* Taking steps toward your goals turns dreams into reality.
- *Awaken Your Inner Pup:* Recognize and nurture your inner strengths and talents.
- *Abundance is Your Birthright:* Believe that you deserve abundance in all areas of your life.

B's: Be-Attitudes: Cultivating a Life of Champ-like Qualities

Inspired by the teachings of the Beatitudes, the Be-Attitudes illuminate the path to living a life of Champ-like qualities. By cultivating thankfulness, forgiveness, and kindness, we open ourselves to the transformative power of love and unlock the door to true happiness.

- *Be Grateful:* Appreciate all your experiences, both good and bad, as they shape who you are. Wag your tail at life!
- *Be a Peacemaker:* Foster unity and harmony in your interactions. No growling allowed!
- *Be Patient:* Trust that everything happens in divine timing. Sometimes, you just have to wait for that *pawfect* treat.
- *Be Loving:* Show unconditional love to yourself and others. Share those belly rubs!
- *Be Forgiving:* Let go of grudges, especially towards yourself. Roll over and let it go.
- *Be Compassionate:* Practice the highest form of unconditional love through empathy and kindness. Give those comforting licks.
- *Be Pawsitive:* Spread your light and *pawsitivity* to those around you. Be the sunshine on a rainy day.

- *Be Serving:* Open yourself to serve a *pawpose,* and your *pawpose* will find you. Fetch for the greater good.

C's: Champ-like Actions to Overcome Challenges: Embracing Resilience and Change

These principles encourage us to take control of our lives, shift our *pawspectives,* and act with courage and compassion. By following these Champ-like actions, we can overcome obstacles and embrace resilience and change. Here are the C's to guide you:

- *Choose to Take Control of Your Actions:* Empower yourself by taking responsibility for your life. Be the leader of your pack.
- *Change Your Pawspective, Change Your World:* Shift your mindset to transform your reality. Sniff out the silver linings.
- *Communicate Your Feelings:* Express your emotions honestly and openly. Don't keep those barks bottled up.
- *Compassion is Divine Love:* Show deep, unconditional love and understanding. Offer a paw of support.
- *Commit to Your Destiny:* Stay dedicated to your path and goals. Follow your nose to your dreams.
- *Create from Your Heart:* Let your actions and creations stem from genuine passion and love. Dig deep and find your passion.
- *Courage Builds Confidence:* Brave actions build self-assurance. Face those fire hydrants head-on.
- *Confidence Empowers You:* Belief in yourself propels you forward. Strut your stuff!
- *Contribute to Others:* Share your gifts and talents to make a *pawsitive* impact. Fetch for a cause.
- *Celebrate Your Wins, Big and Small:* Celebrate your achievements, like finding that perfect stick, no matter how tiny.

Pawsitive Application: Living the ABCs, Doggie Style

To truly live the ABCs of a champion's life, you gotta *fetch* these principles into your daily routine. While it's essential to incorporate all of Champ's teachings, we'll review a few key ways to master these ideas in your everyday life. Start by identifying small, *barkable* steps you can take each day. Whether it's setting aside time for reflection, practicing mindfulness, or taking intentional actions that align with these principles, consistency is key. Keep a *pup journal* to track your progress and reflect on your experiences. Celebrate your successes and learn from your challenges.

Here are three tips to help you develop awareness, acceptance, and action:

- **Tip #1: Awareness—Sniff Out Mindfulness**
  Start each day with a few moments of mindful sniffing. Pay attention to your thoughts, feelings, and surroundings. Notice without judgment and embrace the present moment.

- **Tip #2: Acceptance—Wag and Let Go**
  Practice accepting things as they are. This doesn't mean you have to like or agree with everything; it means you recognize the reality of the situation. Acceptance can lead to peace and clarity. It's like wagging your tail even when it rains on your walk.

- **Tip #3: Action—Fetch Your Goals**
  Focus on consistent, small actions that align with your larger goals. Even tiny paw steps can lead to significant progress over time. Keep moving forward, no matter how small the step. Keep fetching that ball!

Here are three suggestions to help you practice gratitude, compassion and *pawsitivity:*

- **Suggestion 1: Gratitude—Tail-Wagging Thanks**
  Keep a gratitude journal. Write down three things you're grateful for each day. This practice shifts your focus from what's lacking to what's abundant in your life. Wag your tail for all the good stuff.

- **Suggestion 2: Compassion—Paws for Kindness**
  Show compassion to yourself and others. Practice self-care and

extend kindness to those around you. Remember, small acts of kindness can have a big impact.

- **Suggestion 3: Pawsitivity—Be the Sunshine**
  Surround yourself with *pawsitive* influences. Limit exposure to negative media and engage in activities that uplift your spirit. Affirm *pawsitive* beliefs about yourself and your capabilities. Be the sunshine on a cloudy day.

Two simple ways to build confidence and courage:

- **Confidence: Strut Your Stuff:** Confidence builds with practice and *pawsitive* reinforcement. Challenge yourself to step out of your comfort zone regularly. Acknowledge and celebrate your achievements, no matter how small.

- **Courage: Face the Fire Hydrants:** Courage is not the absence of fear but taking action despite it. Embrace challenges as opportunities for growth. Remember, each step forward builds your courage muscle, no matter how small.

Ideas to help you commit to personal growth and contributing to others:

- **Idea #1: Personal Growth—Wag and Learn**
  Commit to lifelong learning and self-improvement. Read books, attend workshops, and seek out mentors who inspire you. Set aside time for personal development each week. Keep wagging and learning.

- **Idea #2: Contributing to Others—Fetch for a Cause**
  Find ways to give back to your community. Volunteer your time, share your skills, or simply be there for someone in need. Contribution enriches your life and fosters a sense of *pawpose*. Fetch for a cause and make a difference.

Adding these strategies to your daily routine will make living the ABCs as natural as a wagging tail. Applying Champ's wisdom helps you tap into your true *pawtential* and live your best life. Embrace these ideas, and let the journey of *pawsformation* begin!

Wagging Tails and Wrapping Up the ABCs: Living the Life of a Champ

Living the ABCs of a Champ is a transformative journey that reshapes your life. Embracing these ideas leads to profound personal growth and fulfillment.

Every paw forward you take to implement these concepts brings you closer to living a doggone happy life with *pawpose*. It's the small, consistent actions that create lasting change. By committing to these practices, you unlock your true *pawtential* and become a beacon of light.

Embrace the ABCs of living the life of a Champ and let them guide you toward a meaningful life. Let Champ's joyful spirit and unwavering determination inspire you every day. Your challenges will become stepping stones to a brighter future.

As we wag on to the next chapter, we'll explore the deep connection Champ and I shared. We'll dig into the spiritual bond between humans and dogs and how it shapes our lives. I'll share 'tails' that reveal the heart of our bond and how you can *fetch* the wisdom of your furry friend to enrich your life.

Grab a treat, pat your furry friend, and get ready for the next adventure. Guided by Champ's enduring spirit, we'll *sniff out* the mysteries of this spiritual journey. With each page, we will celebrate the joy and wisdom our dogs bring into our lives, ensuring their lessons live on in our hearts forever. Stay tuned as we continue this expedition, honoring the incredible bond that makes dogs our true best friends.

CHAPTER 04

TAILS AND TALES: THE SPIRITUAL BOND BETWEEN HUMANS AND DOGS

If you're like me, your relationship with your dog goes beyond words—a magical, almost magnetic connection. *That's* the bond Champ and I shared. Champ wasn't just a companion; he was my confidant and soul partner in life's adventures. His presence was transformative, touching every aspect of my life.

In many ways, our bond mirrored the deep connections I've encountered in my work with twin flames—a term used to describe two souls who are mirror images of each other. It felt like Champ and I were destined to find each other, brought together by a force beyond our understanding, much like twin flames.

Throughout this chapter, we'll dig into the spiritual aspects of our bond, from telepathic communication and shared energy to the profound understanding that flowed between us. You'll discover how our connection exemplifies the broader human-canine relationship and how dogs can be both healers and spiritual guides. We'll also explore stories beyond just Champ and me, highlighting how this connection continues even after our furry friends cross the rainbow bridge.

So, find a comfy spot, snuggle up with your furry friend, and let's dive into the spiritual world of the human-canine bond.

The Mystical Human-Canine Bond: Unleashing Spiritual Connections

Our connection with our canine companions transcends the scientific bond—it's more a spiritual marvel. As we dig into this bond, we uncover the intertwined threads of telepathy, empathy, and a unified journey of growth and understanding.

In spirituality, dogs have long been revered as mystical beings, guardians of the soul. Champ embodied this role with grace and devotion. Some may call it a coincidence, but I firmly believe that Champ was my *familiar*—a supernatural entity guiding me on my journey, offering protection and insight.

As I reflect on the intricacies of our spiritual relationship, one aspect that continually astounds me is the phenomenon of telepathy—a form of communication that transcends the limitations of spoken language. Champ and I shared a profound telepathic bond that defied rational explanation.

The bond between Champ and me was unbreakable—or so I thought. But life had a cruel twist for us, one that would test the limits of our love, stability, and communication.

I planned my life around sharing Champ with my ex-life partner, because I knew I never wanted to be the one not to see or be with Champ. I lived in the same area to avoid taking Champ away from him. But little did I know that he had been conspiring to take Champ from me.

It began with a phone call just 13 seconds long, yet shattered my world into a million pieces. My ex-life partner, whom I once trusted with my heart, uttered words piercing my soul like a dagger. *"I'm done trading the dog with you,"* he said coldly. *"I want you out of my life." "This is the last time you will ever hear from me." Click!*

In that moment, time stood still. I was paralyzed, unable to comprehend the magnitude of what had just transpired. Champ, my soulmate, was being ripped away, and I could do nothing to stop it.

It was such a shock because there had been no conflict; I shared Champ with him for three years. But now, in the blink of an eye, he was gone, snatched away by the very person who had once loved and cherished both of us.

The pain of separation was unbearable for Champ and me. We were two halves of a whole, torn apart and left to navigate the world alone. Nights turned into days and days into weeks, but the ache in my heart never dulled. I could feel Champ's absence like a gaping hole in my soul, a void nothing could fill.

Yet, amidst the darkness, a glimmer of hope remained. I refused to accept defeat, determined to fight for Champ with every fiber of my being. And so, the legal battle began—a grueling, uphill struggle that tested my strength and resolve.

This extraordinary connection became particularly evident during this separation. Despite the physical distance between us, Champ remained a constant presence in my life, his spirit reaching out to comfort and reassure me in my darkest moments.

Yet, the journey to reunite with Champ brought out my fears and challenges, testing my ability to survive. In the face of skepticism and indifference from authorities, I was forced to confront the harsh reality of logistics and red tape. I would have folded if Champ hadn't been on the other side of this battle because enduring it all was excruciating.

Right after Champ was taken from me, I reported it to the police, only to be laughed at. I was told that dogs are property and that because he was the one who had Champ, I might as well hang up the idea of getting him back. One officer even told me that even if I was awarded Champ in court and had documents signed by the judge, he still would not go to retrieve Champ for me.

Nevertheless, I was determined to get Champ back. The journey was long and taxing, involving multiple attorneys and a court trial that made history in our county. Champ's spirit kept me going. His presence empowered me, teaching me to find my voice and fight for what was right.

Finally, after eight long months of uncertainty and anguish, the moment of reunion arrived. Champ was returned to me, his eyes shining with recognition and unforgettable love. The world's weight lifted from my shoulders as I held him in my arms once more, feeling his heartbeat against mine.

In our reunion, I found solace and redemption—a reminder that love conquers all, even in the darkest times. And as we forged ahead, hand in paw, I knew we could overcome any obstacle together.

I understood that Champ was helping me free myself of my past and that I was not to continue putting my life on hold. The Divine had meticulously planned every part of our difficult journey for me to gain personal lessons and soul freedom.

Ultimately, our telepathic connection was a guiding light, leading me through the darkness and reuniting us. Love and determination can conquer all.

Pawsitive Telepathy: Mind-Melding with Your Mutt

Through telepathy, I stayed connected with Champ's spirit. I could sense his emotions and receive guidance during uncertain times. Many who have shared a profound connection with their pets experience this telepathic bond, even after their pet has passed.

I vividly recall one time when I felt unsure about Champ's return. I worked online with a client, helping her find peace with losing her beloved cat, Miss Kitty. As I guided Miss Kitty through her transition, Champ's presence suddenly filled the room. His gentle voice echoed in my mind with reassurance: *"Don't worry, Momma, it's okay. I will be back. Look at the picture of me in the living room; I have a message to show you I will return."*

Still in session, I went to the living room for the photo. When I looked at the picture, it was of Champ appearing to meditate with a quote by the Dalai Lama: *"Don't let the behavior of others rob you of your inner peace."* At that moment, a calmness washed over me, and I knew my fur baby would return.

Let's paws and reflect on the amazing ways our pets communicate with us beyond words, wagging their way into our hearts and minds, offering comfort and guidance from the great beyond.

Spiritual Sniffing: Dogs as Guides to Healing

Dogs lead us on the path to spiritual growth. With his gentle presence and unwavering love, Champ played a key role in my journey of healing and self-discovery.

Champ wasn't just a fur-mate but my co-healer during client energy healing sessions. As an energy healer, his breath would synchronize with mine, and he could sense and shift the client's energy, helping in their healing process. Together, we explored the realms of healing for people worldwide.

I was often amazed by Champ's *intuitive abilities*. He knew when I needed healing and offered support at just the right moments. Sometimes, I could even hear his voice, guiding me with wisdom beyond his physical presence.

Our spiritual connection was vital during tough times. After my ex-partner took Champ from me, I experienced significant anxiety and stress. Signs and *telepathic messages* reminded me to stay strong and focused on our reunion.

This experience taught me *empowerment*—how to stand up, show up, and speak up for myself. Our connection went beyond words; it was *a silent dialogue between souls.* Champ's thoughts intertwined with mine, his presence a constant reminder of the deeper truths within us all. He became my *spiritual guru.*

Embracing the spiritual relationship with our pets can provide *profound healing and insight.* It reminds us that love is eternal and our bonds with our animals are unbreakable, even in separation. This connection can awaken dormant parts of ourselves and offer a sense of continuity and presence that transcends the physical realm.

Spirit Sniffin': Messages Beyond the Rainbow Bridge

Many dog lovers, including me, have felt a profound connection with their furry friends even after they've crossed the rainbow bridge. This ongoing communication from the spirit world brings immense comfort and guidance, reminding us that love transcends our existence.

When Champ crossed the rainbow bridge, our connection didn't end—it evolved. I experienced moments of profound clarity, often guided by Champ's enduring spirit. This form of communication appeared in various ways, like dreams, sudden insights, or just feeling his presence. For many, these experiences are more than mere coincidences—they're seen as messages from the spirit world.

Champ's presence continued to be felt. Sometimes, I'd find objects related to him appearing unexpectedly or hear his familiar sounds in quiet moments. These signs often came when I needed comfort or reassurance, reminding me he was still by my side, guiding me through life's challenges.

Learning to communicate with Champ on a spiritual level also taught me to communicate with other animals. Clients began seeking my assistance to energetically heal and communicate with their pets, which helped animals transition peacefully.

One day, while writing this chapter, I visited my Facebook page and found a message from a friend. After Champ's passing, she commented on a picture I posted of Champ and me:

> *"Love never leaves us, and neither does the joy we shared. It just changes forms."*

I responded:

> *"Yes, these big-hearted souls get to expand their presence."*

Later, I returned to find her response, too synchronistic not to share:

> *"Yes, these big-hearted souls get to expand their presence. I feel our dogs on The Magicland (where her Treehouse resides) and know our other animals and guests do as well. This is the first time I've shared this story. We had a family who had stayed in our Treehouse a few times. They were excited to return—the son was about five and very active. Mom kept reminding him to hold the railing on the stairs. He accidentally left the sliding glass door open and forgot. So when he went to lean back on the door, he tumbled down the stairs as his father watched in horror, knowing he would not be okay by the time his end-over-end event landed at the bottom of the stairs. Mom messaged me, saying they were headed to the ER, apologizing for what happened and taking full responsibility. He was 100% okay. They did tests to be sure and said, take it easy. I was in deep prayer. I set up a big swinging chair, fuzzy blankets, and stuffed animals for him and his little sister and took up newborn chicks so they could all find joy and delight. Dad was still shaken up. Dad told his son, 'Tell Laura Lynne what you said happened.' I thought he would share the details; the little boy said this instead. As he fell backward, he pointed to the exact spot his dog (who had passed away) was standing and said his dog ran to him and cushioned his fall so he was safe! He continued, 'I believe The Magicland is where all dogs come to when they pass away.' He was held by the love of*

the spirit of the animals and was safe. Our gratitude abounds, and his ability to see and know the angel dogs was amazing."

As we honor these connections, we open ourselves to the wisdom and love our pets continue to offer from the spirit world.

Soulful Connections: Everyday Moments with Champ

Reflecting on Champ's everyday presence, I am reminded of how deeply intertwined our souls became. Champ was my shadow and protector. His presence filled even the smallest moments with joy and warmth.

When Champ arrived in my life, he made it clear that he needed to always be near me. Whether I was working at my desk, lounging on the couch, or even using the bathroom, Champ was there, his watchful gaze never straying far from mine. This need to be close wasn't out of dependence but a testament to our deep bond. Champ intuitively understood my moods and emotions, making it his mission to protect me and offer comfort in times of distress.

Champ's ability to sense my thoughts and feelings before I knew them was one of the most remarkable aspects of our connection. Countless times, I would find myself lost in thought, only to be jolted back to reality by Champ's gentle nudge or soulful gaze, as if to say, *"Hey, I'm here for you, Momma."*

Champ was always one step ahead during our everyday activities, anticipating my needs and desires with uncanny accuracy. Whether it was letting me know it was time for bed or offering a sympathetic paw when I was feeling down, Champ had an innate knack for lifting my spirits and bringing a smile to my heart. He was my furry alarm clock and emotional support, all rolled into one adorable package.

The most profound moments of connection occurred during our quiet, reflective times together. Sitting in companionable silence, I could feel Champ's presence like a warm embrace, soothing my troubled mind and filling me with peace. In Champ, I found solitude and a kindred spirit who understood me in a way no one else could. Our everyday connection was a testament to the power of love, reminding me that the most profound bonds are often forged in the simplest moments.

As we continue this journey, cherish those tail-wagging, heartwarming moments with your furry friends. They remind you that true friendship is found in everyday interactions and our dogs' unconditional love.

Shared Pawpose: Changing the World with Love and Compassion

The bond between humans and their pets goes beyond friendship; it's a partnership working to improve the world. Our pets, with their loyal and loving nature, show us the true meaning of humility and compassion, spiritual qualities that help us master the Divine within ourselves.

When Champ and I joined forces, he brought a special mission. His gentle presence and deep understanding reminded me we had a greater *pawpose.* We weren't just pet and owner; we were partners on a journey of love and healing, striving each day to improve the world.

Champ had a mission, and I realized my role was to help share that mission with the world. By telling our story, I shared his *wisdom* and *spirit.* Champ's message touched many hearts, showing people that their pets are not just animals but partners in a journey of love and growth.

Through my interactions with Champ, I learned more about *humility* and *compassion.* He taught me that true strength comes from *kindness* and that even small acts of love can make a big difference. Together, we aimed to change not just our own lives but also the lives of others, creating a *wave of love* that spread far and wide.

Champ's message lives on, inspiring people and pets everywhere. His *mission of love and transformation* continues, encouraging everyone to *be a light* in the world. Our shared *pawpose,* driven by deep *love,* shows the remarkable impact we can have when working with our pets to improve the world.

As we move forward, remember that every moment with our pets is a chance to learn, grow, and spread love. Together, we can change the world, one heart at a time, guided by the humility and compassion our beloved pets show us daily.

Wrapping Up the Woof-tastic Spiritual Journey

In closing, I am reminded of Anatole France's words: "Until one has loved an animal, a part of one's soul remains unawakened." With Champ as my guide and confidant, I have awakened to the boundless beauty and wonder of our spiritual bond with our dogs.

Through Champ, I learned the power of unconditional love—the kind that transcends boundaries, time, and distance. This love touched the core of my being, awakening parts of myself that had long lain dormant. As we explore the depths of this bond, I invite you to reflect on your spiritual connection with your canine companion. Perhaps, like me, you've experienced moments of profound harmony where words are unnecessary, and love speaks volumes.

As you think about the wagging tails and soulful eyes that greet you daily, remember the silent promises and unspoken wisdom our dogs share. They show us how to live in the now, love fully, and face challenges with courage and a wagging tail.

Now, grab a treat, pat your furry friend, and prepare for the next adventure. It's time to meet the Mighty Staffy's breed that exemplifies strength and power. We'll unleash how these remarkable dogs face challenges and stereotypes with courage and determination, becoming ambassadors of hope.

CHAPTER 05

MEET THE MIGHTY STAFFY: OVERCOMING RUFFS AND RUMBLES

Get ready to dive into the 'tail' of the Staffordshire Bull Terrier, or "Staffies" (also spelled "Staffys"), as we affectionately call them. Imagine a superhero with a wagging tail, combining strength and agility. These dogs are not just muscle and might; they are bundles of joy wrapped in fur, ready to win hearts with every smile.

In this chapter, we'll explore the history and evolution of these noble pooches, from their early days in England, where they were known as the *Bull-and-Terrier Dog,* to their journey to America, where they became the beloved "Staffies" we know today. Highlighting their transformation from fighters to lovers shows how their courage and inner strength have defined them as a breed.

Beyond history lessons and pedigree charts, we'll sniff out the stereotypes and misconceptions surrounding bully breeds. You'll meet some of Champ's bully breed buddies who have faced adversity head-on and come out with tails wagging. Through *The Triumph Tails Survey,* their stories of resilience and courage will shed light on the true spirit of these dogs. Their journeys of overcoming ruffs and rumbles will warm your heart and inspire you to see the incredible potential within every dog—and maybe within yourself, too.

47

Unleashing the Truth: Staffy vs. Pitbull – The Tail-Wagging Tale

Most folks in America often bark up the wrong tree by mistaking Staffies for Pitbulls. Staffies, like Champ, come from England and are a blend of the strong English Bulldog and the spry Manchester Terrier. The *English Bulldog* brings muscle, while the *Manchester Terrier* adds a zippy energy. Pitbulls usually have longer legs, while Champ sports shorter, sturdier ones, making them a compact bundle of joy and strength.

The Staffordshire Bull Terrier eventually pawed its way into becoming its own breed and was brought to America in the early 19th century. Initially, these dogs were called *Bull-and-Terrier Dogs, Half and Half, or Pit Dogs.* Later, they proudly took on the name Staffordshire Bull Terriers in England. The breed was officially recognized by The Kennel Club in the UK in 1935 and by the American Kennel Club (AKC) in 1974. Once in America, these Staffies were mixed with other dogs to create the American Staffordshire Terrier, or Am Staffs, thus creating a distinct bully breed.

In America, the Am Staffs mixed with various breeds, leading to the creation of the *American Pit Bull Terrier,* the "classic" Pit Bull we know today. Champ's breed, the Staffordshire Bull Terrier, is often considered the granddaddy of the Pit Bull. Pit Bulls have been bred more for their attitude and temperament than their looks, resulting in a delightful mix of shapes and sizes. Originally bred as fighting dogs, they are a mix of bulldogs, mastiffs, and terriers, combining size, strength, agility, and determination. Any aggressive nature in them comes from these mixed breeds and, of course, how they are raised and the training they receive from their owners. They also tend to take on the energy of their owner, which is why it's crucial to be a responsible bully breed owner.

Staffordshire Bull Terriers are renowned for their great courage and inner spirit. They're brilliant and very affectionate—I call it *bully affectionate.* These dogs wear their hearts on their sleeves (or, rather, their faces), and humans can always read what they're thinking. Oh, and they absolutely adore little people! They've earned the nickname *Nanny Dog,* as they are fantastic family pets. They love exercise but aren't as hyper as some of their relatives. Their determination, goal orientation, and focus require owners who understand them and direct their energy *pawsitively.*

Champ's journey is a testament to the resilience inherent in Staffordshire Bull Terriers. His legacy is of overcoming challenges and embracing change, teaching us valuable lessons about bravery and inner power. One of the key messages we shared with people through Champ's social media was the importance of understanding and challenging stereotypes about bully breeds. His story of navigating ruffs and rumbles—both literally and metaphorically—illustrates the strength and heart these dogs possess. One of the most significant ways I supported Champ was by being a voice for his cause.

Rumbles and Realities: Educating About Bully Breed Stereotypes

Dogs will be dogs, just like kids will be kids, and humans will be humans. Should we all get the same punishment for just being who we are? Shouldn't we be judged based on our actions? A common saying among bully breed advocates is, *"Punish the deed, not the breed."* While some people believe that mixing breeds can lead to more aggressive temperaments, this isn't specific to any one breed. In reality, temperament depends on many factors, including genetics, environment, and training. Bully breeds, like any other dogs, can be loving and gentle companions when raised in a *pawsitive* environment.

That's why Champ and I made it our mission to help educate humans. It's essential to understand that training should be based on the individual dog, not the breed. Owners need to take responsibility for their actions and their dogs' behavior. The misconceptions aren't just about a lack of education on breed-specific regulations; they stem from personal beliefs and *pawspectives* as well. By challenging these stereotypes, we can create a more understanding and compassionate world for all breeds.

Bully breeds deal with these misconceptions daily. The tragic story of Lennox, a dog in Belfast, Northern Ireland, who was euthanized just for being a bully breed, struck a chord with me. It took me a couple of years to realize the weight my dog, Champ, carried simply because of his breed. I couldn't stand the idea that if another aggressive dog attacked him, Champ could be the one in trouble just because of his breed.

To achieve true freedom for bully breeds—and all breeds—we must work beyond global, country, state, and local regulations to end breed-specific laws. If we want global bully breed freedom and personal freedom for individuals, we need to address the root causes: human actions and beliefs.

Humans must examine their actions and beliefs that lead to these regulations. By understanding and challenging these misconceptions, we can create a world where dogs are judged by their deeds, not their breeds.

In the next chapter, we will review *The Howl and Growl Survey,* a study exploring why humans judge bully breeds and the misconceptions they hold. Now, let's hear from some incredible dogs who have overcome judgment and adversity in *The Triumph Tails Survey.*

Triumphs of Champ's Bully Breed Friends: The Triumph Tails Survey

In this section, we share inspiring stories of some of Champ's bully-breed BFFs who have faced and overcome significant challenges. Through *The Triumph Tails Survey,* these incredible dogs share their experiences, the lessons they've learned, and the wisdom they've gained along the way. Their 'tails' highlight the qualities that define the bully breed. Each dog offers unique insights and advice on focusing on the *pawsitive,* overcoming adversities, and living a life full of *pawpose* and joy. Let their journeys inspire you to see beyond the surface and embrace the true *pawtential* within yourself and others.

Here are just a few of the responses we got from *The Triumph Tails Survey:*

Ruger's Journey with Epilepsy

- *What challenges have you overcome?* I live with epilepsy. I had my first seizure just before my fourth birthday. There's no history of epilepsy in my family, so the dog-tors called it idiopathic epilepsy, which means they don't know why it happens.

- *What have you learned from your challenges?* With great pawrents who never gave up, I learned to keep going and enjoy every day because it could be my last. My pawrents always look for new treatments and research to help me.

- *How do you share your lessons with others?* I have a Facebook page where I raise awareness about canine epilepsy. I shared a video of myself having a seizure to help other pet owners recognize the signs. I also post resources on first aid, diet, and living happily with epilepsy. My motto is, *"There are no disabilities, only ignorance and bad attitudes."*

- *What advice do you have for humans to stay pawsitive?* Turn negative experiences into *pawsitives.* On the anniversary of my first seizure, instead of being sad, my dad and I started *Ruger's Paws—A Day of Kindness to Others.* Many friends joined in, making it a day of joy instead of sorrow.

Willing's Story of Overcoming Physical Challenges

- *What challenges have you overcome?* I was born with only three legs and have no "good" legs. One leg was amputated, another is a peg leg, and I have elbow dysplasia and a fused spine. But my mom says I'm *pawfect!*

- *What have you learned from your challenges?* There are no real obstacles, just the limits we set. Despite my physical issues, I live a happy life.

- *How do you share your lessons with others?* I'm a therapy dog. I visit elderly people in rehab centers and kids in elementary school reading programs. I show people that no matter their condition, they can still bring joy and make a difference.

- *What advice do you have for humans to stay pawsitive?* Focus on what you can do, not what you can't. Your limitations are only in your mind. Embrace your *impawfections* and use them to connect with and inspire others. *Pawfection* is about finding joy and *pawpose* in your life, not being flawless.

Ginger's Triumph Over Neglect

- *What challenges have you overcome?* I was abandoned and neglected. When I was rescued, I was malnourished and scared. I didn't trust humans, but with time and love, I healed.

- *What have you learned from your challenges?* Love and kindness can heal even the deepest wounds. With *pawtience* and tender care, I found some good humans who want to help and love us.

- *How do you share your lessons with others?* I became an ambassador for rescue dogs, showing that even those with *ruff* starts can become loving companions. My story is shared in forums and on social media, inspiring others to adopt and give second chances to dogs in need.

- *What advice do you have for humans to stay pawsitive?* Your past doesn't define you. The love and support you receive help shape your future. Building trust and spreading kindness will create a better world for yourself and those around you.

Celebrating the Triumphs of Champ and His Bully Breed BFFs

As we close this chapter, let's *paws* for a moment to celebrate the incredible resilience and bravery demonstrated by bully breeds.

Reflecting on these journeys, we see the power of education and awareness in changing *pawceptions* and celebrating the unique qualities of bully breeds. Let's carry forward the lessons of courage and resilience as we continue our mission to become ambassadors for these incredible companions.

Alright, pack! We've seen how mighty Staffies tackle ruffs and rumbles. Now, let's wag our way into understanding why humans judge. In the next chapter, *Why Humans Judge: Insights from the Howl and Growl Survey,* we'll sniff out the reasons behind human judgment and uncover some *pawsitive* lessons from our furry friends' *pawspectives.*

CHAPTER 06

WHY HUMANS JUDGE: INSIGHTS FROM THE HOWL AND GROWL SURVEY

One of my favorite quotes by my long-time mentor, the late Dr. Wayne Dyer, is, "*When you judge another, you do not define them; you define yourself.*" We all know people judge, but why? This has been the question I've spent most of my life trying to answer. Growing up in a strict religious home, I felt the weight of judgment constantly. It took many years to stop judging myself and break free from those expectations.

Champ and I share a joint mission: to end judgment, especially against bully breeds. My experiences with feeling judged deeply resonated with Champ's mission to challenge these stereotypes. To better understand why people judge, I posed the question on Champ's Facebook page, my own, and asked everyone I met who was willing to share their thoughts. The response was overwhelming—101 answers! Here are the top five reasons people gave for why they judge:

1. *Belief Systems* – what they were taught.
2. *Ego* – the need to be right or in control.
3. *Fear* – afraid to let go and afraid of change.
4. *Protection* – putting up walls to not get hurt.
5. *Holding Grudges* – the inability to forgive.

Now, we will dig into why life sometimes feels heavy and burdensome. In this chapter, we'll explore the underlying reasons that weigh us down—like judgment, ego, and fear—and how these hidden obstacles can block our path to joy. Just as Champ loves uncovering hidden treasures in his blanket after burying his bones, understanding these reasons helps us let go of them and find the new, exciting things that bring lightness and joy into our lives. We'll also share practical ways to reprogram these outdated beliefs and judgments, allowing us to create a lighter, more fulfilling life.

So, get comfy, grab a treat (or two), and we'll dig into why people judge. By the end of this chapter, you'll feel lighter and have a few more wagging tails of joy in your life.

Judgment #1: Burying Old Bones: Letting Go of Outdated Belief Systems

It took me a while to understand that I'm not defined by my parents' fears and beliefs. Old thoughts and prejudices get passed down like a family heirloom no one wants. These thoughts sit deep in our minds, becoming our belief systems, like inheriting a bunch of dusty, old bones you didn't even bury yourself.

To understand our actions, we need to understand our belief systems. We can start thinking for ourselves when we let go of old beliefs that no longer help us. Like Champ burying old bones and finding new treasures, we can clear out the old to make way for the new.

We often need to examine our past and release what's holding us back to move forward. Our memories and experiences are stored in our minds and every cell of our bodies. Letting go of outdated habits and beliefs is like cleaning out a closet filled with clothes that no longer fit. Imagine still wearing fashion from the '80s—yikes! It's time to clear out the old and make space for something new and transformative.

This process of letting go is like a cleansing ritual. It lightens and brightens our inner space, making room for healthier habits that bring more joy. Just as Champ eagerly buried his bone, excited about the treasures he'd uncover, we too can enjoy embracing new, empowering beliefs. Picture finding that *pawfect* outfit that makes you feel fabulous—now imagine doing the same for your mind and spirit, creating clarity and living with more joy and less judgment. *In Trick #1,* Champ will guide you on how to bury your old bones—letting go of what no longer serves you, from habits to emotional and physical baggage. To help you start this journey, here are some *pawsitive* steps to help you begin letting go of old beliefs:

- **Sniff Out the Source:** Just like a dog sniffs out hidden treasures, take a moment to trace back where your old beliefs come from. Are they hand-me-downs from your family, like those dusty old bones? Once you identify them, you can start deciding which ones to keep and which to bury for good.

- **Dig Up and Bury:** It's time to do some digging! Just as Champ would bury his old bones to make space for new ones, identify those outdated beliefs, and let them go. Picture yourself burying those old thoughts that no longer serve you, making room for fresh, empowering ones.

- **Fetch New Beliefs:** Once you've buried the old, it's time to fetch some new beliefs! Imagine running through a field, excitedly discovering new ideas that better align with who you are now. These are the bones worth keeping that bring joy, growth, and a wagging tail.

- **Wag Your Tail with Gratitude:** After you've done the work, take a moment to wag your tail in gratitude. Celebrate the progress you've made and the new beliefs you've embraced. Just like a dog showing appreciation, give yourself a mental pat on the back for the hard work of reprogramming your mind.

Judgment #2: Dropping the Alpha Act: Letting Go of Ego

The ego is like that loud, barking dog in your head that thinks it's the boss of everything. Understanding ego means recognizing it as a false sense of reality and identity based on external factors. It's the voice telling you that you need the fanciest toys, the best treats, and the biggest doghouse to be happy. But we all know deep down that a good belly rub and a warm place to sleep are what really matter.

A healthy ego helps us navigate daily life, like knowing when it's your turn to fetch the ball. *But an out-of-control ego?* That's like a dog who won't stop barking at its own reflection. On the other hand, the spiritual self knows that true happiness comes from within and that life is more about wagging tails than hoarding toys.

There's an inner battle between the ego self and the spiritual self. Visualize playing tug-of-war inside your mind: one side is the ego, insisting, *"I need to be right, I need to be better!"* while the other side, your spiritual self, is calmly saying, *"Hey, let's enjoy the sunshine and be grateful for the treats we have."*

Pawsitive Practices to Transcend Ego

- **Approach Conflicts with Peace and Understanding:** Instead of barking back when someone growls at you, try to understand where they're coming from. They may have had a *ruff* day and need a little *pawtience.*

- **Put Yourself in Others' Paws:** Imagine how walking a mile in another dog's paws feels. Empathy can go a long way in dissolving ego-driven conflicts.

- **Let Go of the Notion That Everything Is Personal:** Not every growl is about you. It might just be a bad day at the park. Learn to let things roll off your back like water off a duck.

- **Remove Competition and the Need for Superiority:** Life isn't always about being the top dog. Letting someone else fetch the ball can be the kindest thing you can do. Winning every race isn't necessary; enjoying the run is what matters.

- **Overcome the Desire for Ego-Based Accomplishments:** Achievements are outstanding, but if they're driven by ego, they can lead to a never-ending chase. Actual accomplishments bring joy and fulfillment, like finally digging up that hidden bone.

Taming the ego is like training a puppy. It takes patience, consistency, and a lot of love. When we release the need to always be right or the best, we open ourselves to true treasures—meaningful relationships, inner peace, and the simple joys of life.

It's time to drop the alpha act and embrace our spiritual self. Approach life with a wagging tail, ready to appreciate the real treasures around us.

Judgment #3: Fear? Fur-get About It—Letting Go of Fear

Fear is like that mysterious vacuum cleaner in the corner—loud, scary, and paralyzing if you let it be. The fear of change can stop us in our tracks, just like a cat frozen in front of a cucumber. *But what if I told you that fear is nothing more than an illusion created by our ego?* It's like barking at the mailman every day, thinking he's a threat when, really, he's just bringing goodies. Practicing the following ideas can help you fur-get about your fear:

- **Fear of Change—A Common and Paralyzing Concern:** We don't always like our circumstances, but the thought of change can be terrifying. Even if it's worn out and full of holes, holding onto what we know can be comforting, much like sticking with an old, frayed chew toy while ignoring the new, shiny one right next to it.

- **Fear is an Illusion Produced by Ego:** Fear can be like a warning from your ego, cautioning you about the *pawtential* discomfort of a new toy. It tricks us into thinking that bad things will happen, using scare tactics to keep us stuck. When we let fear and ego take over, we miss out on the fun, just like avoiding a new toy because it might squeak in an unpleasant way.

- **Shift Your Pawception to Find Peace Within Stressful Situations:** Changing how we *pawceive* stressful situations can help us find peace. Envision looking at a thunderstorm and, instead of being scared, thinking about how it waters the plants and fills the rivers. It's all about seeing the silver lining—or the silver bone.

- **The Physical and Mental Impact of Fear:** Hanging onto fear can make it feel like something scary has already happened. This keeps us in a state of anxiety and can even make us sick. Fear in the mind manifests in the body, causing paralysis in our actions and lives. Imagine being too scared to fetch because you think the stick might bite back.

- **Identify and Meet Fears Head-On to Move Forward in Life:** To move forward, we must identify and face our fears head-on. Translate their meaning and see what might be lacking in yourself, causing the anxiety. Think about a shadow on the wall, realizing it's just a trick of the light and deciding it's not so intimidating after all.

Now, it's time to explore the importance of lowering our guard and understanding why self-protection might hold us back.

Judgment #4: Guard Down, Paws Up, Letting Down Your Guard and the Need for Self-Protection

We often put up our guard to avoid conflict, like a dog barking at the UPS driver to keep him at bay. But what if putting up our guard is just making life harder? We need to learn how to *wag more and bark less.*

When we feel threatened, we naturally want to protect ourselves. We build walls *higher than a squirrel's hiding place,* thinking it'll keep us safe. But all this does is keep us from enjoying the park, and we miss out on new experiences and connections.

Examples of How to Approach Situations Without Conflict

Instead of barking at every passerby, approach situations calmly and open-mindedly. Here are some dog-inspired tips:

- **Wag First, Bark Later:** Give people the benefit of the doubt. Maybe they're just having a bad day. Approach with kindness and see how things turn out.

- **Sniff It Out:** Before reacting, take a moment to understand the situation, just like how dogs sniff each other to get acquainted. Try to see things from the other person's *pawspective.*

- **Pawsitive Reinforcement:** Use *pawsitive* communication. Instead of growling, try wagging your tail and offering a friendly gesture. It might just change the whole vibe.

The Emotional Impact of Past Hurts and the Need for Protection

Past hurts can make us want to put up even more walls. Maybe another dog snapped at you, or you stepped on a sharp rock. These experiences make us wary. But holding onto that hurt only keeps us from finding new playmates and adventures. Healing from these past hurts is like learning to *play fetch all over again*—it takes time and patience. Here's how to start:

- **Acknowledge the Hurt:** Recognize the pain and where it's coming from. Admit that the mailman isn't actually a monster.

- **Take Puppy Steps:** Gradually lower your guard. Begin with a slight wag or a cautious sniff.

- **Seek Support:** Just like dogs rely on their pack, lean on friends or family for support. They can help you see things from a new *pawspective.*

The Importance of Setting Appropriate Boundaries and Choosing Battles Wisely

Learning when to let down your guard and when to stand your ground is key. Not every situation requires a *full-on bark*. Sometimes, a gentle woof will do. Here's how to set boundaries:

- **Mark Your Territory:** Know what you're comfortable with and communicate it clearly. Like a dog marking its favorite tree, make your boundaries known.

- **Choose Your Battles:** Not every squirrel is worth chasing. Decide which conflicts are worth your energy and which ones you can let go.

- **Stay Calm and Carry On:** Keep cool even when things get *ruff*. A calm demeanor can defuse most situations.

When we let down our guard, we open ourselves to a world of new *pawssibilities*. By lowering our walls and being open, we can find peace and joy in places we never expected. Discovering that the neighbor's cat isn't an enemy but a *pawtential* friend can be a delightful surprise.

Embracing vulnerability allows us to experience life's joys more fully, forming deeper connections and finding happiness in the little things. Drop your defenses, welcome new experiences, and discover the hidden joys waiting for you.

Judgment #5: Holding Grudges: The Inability to Forgive

Holding onto grudges can be like carrying around a heavy backpack full of rocks. It slows us down and makes life more complicated than it needs to be. *Forgiveness,* on the other hand, lightens our load and frees us to move forward. Mastering *forgiveness* isn't easy, but it's a powerful way to improve our lives and relationships.

Forgiveness doesn't mean forgetting what happened or saying that it was okay. It's about letting go of the anger and hurt so that it doesn't control your life. It's about finding peace within yourself and moving on from the pain.

Doggone Good Steps to Forgive

1. **Sniff Out Your Feelings:** Understand why you're feeling hurt or mad, just like when you sniff around to determine where that strange smell is coming from.

2. **Bark It Out:** Talk to the person who hurt you. Share your feelings calmly, like a friendly bark, and listen to their side. No growling allowed!

3. **Bury It in the Yard:** If talking isn't possible, write down your feelings and bury them like a bone. This helps you process those pesky emotions.

4. **Wag Your Empathy Tail:** Understand why the person acted that way. Maybe they had a bad day and accidentally stepped on a squeaky toy.

5. **Shake Off the Grudge:** Decide to let go of the grudge, just like shaking off after a bath. Focus on the happy times, like when you get belly rubs and treats.

6. **Fetch Some Help:** If it's too *ruff* to forgive alone, talk to someone you trust, like a friend, family member, or your favorite human. They can help you find your way back to tail-wagging happiness.

By practicing these steps, you can learn to master forgiveness, lighten your emotional load, and make room for more joy and *pawsitive* experiences in your life. Remember, *forgiveness* is a gift you give to yourself. It frees you from the past and opens up a brighter future.

Reflecting on Our Journey

Alright pack, let's wag our tails as we look back at what we've learned in this chapter! We've explored why people judge and figured out how to let go of old beliefs, ego, fear, need for self-protection, and shaking off grudges. It's been quite an adventure.

Take a moment to think about your own experiences with judgment and embrace the process of letting go. Remember, it's not about being *pawfect;* it's about making progress and finding joy in the little things.

Where have you been judging? Old beliefs can weigh you down like a pair of heavy boots stuck in the mud, but when you *bury those outdated bones,* you discover new treasures within yourself. Tackling the big, barking ego reveals that true happiness comes from a *wagging tail* and an open heart. Facing your fears head-on shows they are just illusions, like *barking at your reflection.* Letting down your guard to embrace new experiences and connections makes life much more joyful.

Champ found joy in burying and uncovering his bones, each a new adventure. In the same way, we can find happiness by letting go of old judgments and discovering new treasures within ourselves. It's all about the journey, the wagging tails, and the love we share.

As we heal our judgments and empower each other, we create new belief systems that enrich not only our lives but also the lives of bully breeds like Champ. Our mission is much like Mother Teresa's philosophy—focusing on creating peace and unity rather than waging war against what we don't want. This approach, dedicated to promoting compassion and understanding between people and dogs, has earned me the title of the "Mother Teresa of Canines." We can build a world where humans and dogs thrive in harmony by fostering love and acceptance.

Get ready to explore Champ's mission and how his life sparked a global movement of happiness, love, and unity. His wisdom will guide us in spreading joy and making a positive impact on the world, uniting us in a common goal.

In the next chapter, we'll uncover the origins of the *100-Day Smile Challenge,* celebrate its milestones, and see how Champ's legacy continues to inspire smiles and joy worldwide. So, grab your favorite chew toy, find a cozy spot, and continue this tail-wagging adventure!

CHAPTER 07

SPREADING HAPPINESS: CHAMP'S GLOBAL MISSION

Picture a fearless Staffordshire Bull Terrier on a mission to change the world, one smile at a time. That was Champ—a proud representative of a misunderstood breed, determined to break down barriers and melt hearts. Often judged by their appearance rather than their wagging tails and lovable nature, bully breeds like Champ face unfair stigmas.

Champ confidently navigated a world of misconceptions, his tail wagging and smile beaming. He wasn't just any dog; he was a symbol of pawsitivity, challenging stereotypes and spreading happiness wherever he went. Despite society's prejudices, Champ embodied courage and determination, showing the world the true nature of his breed.

His journey was more than just a personal mission—it was a testament to resilience and a beacon of hope in a world filled with judgment. Through Champ's eyes, I witnessed the burden of prejudice he carried. I felt the love and strength that shattered those stereotypes through his heart. Together, we set out to redefine the narrative surrounding bully breeds, proving that a wagging tail and a big smile can change hearts and minds.

In this chapter, we're diving into Champ's incredible *pawpose*. We'll explore the origins of the *100-Day Smile Challenge*, a simple yet powerful gesture that sparked a global movement of love and acceptance, changing how we view bully breeds. Through personal reflections and inspiring anecdotes, we'll uncover the deeper meaning behind Champ's mission and its profound impact on our lives and the world around us.

Get ready for a *tail-wagging adventure* full of smiles and overcoming prejudice, all wrapped up in the warm, furry hug of Champ's legacy.

The 100-Day Tail-Wagging Smile Challenge: Sparking a Movement

It all started with a simple observation: every time Champ and I went for a run, his smile lit up the world around us. This dog, who was supposed to be scary because of his breed, had an incredible ability to make people smile. Strangers would stop us just to say, *"Dude, that is one good-looking dog!"* and their faces would light up with joy. Champ's infectious smile broke down barriers and challenged the stereotypes surrounding him.

At the time, I was going through a challenging period in my life. I felt stuck and needed to end a relationship. But running with Champ gave me a glimpse of hope. Seeing how he made people smile, even when I couldn't, served as a powerful reminder of the impact we can have on others. It seemed Champ was encouraging me, *"Come on, Momma! We've got some smiles to spread!"*

That's when the idea hit me—why not turn this into something bigger? Thus, the *100-Day Smile Challenge* was born. The goal was simple: run for 100 days in a row, and every time Champ made someone smile, we'd stop, gently educate them about his breed, and then post their picture with Champ on his social media page. It was our way of showing the world that dogs like Champ were more than the stereotypes about their breed. They were creatures of warmth and happiness.

The Awakening: Waking Up My Inner Champ

The 100-Day Smile Challenge wasn't just about making others smile; it was a journey of profound personal growth and self-discovery for me, too. At the start, I felt like a dog chasing its own tail, going nowhere fast.

But running with Champ and seeing the joy he brought to others started to change something inside me.

Every smile we inspired became a small victory against the gloom that had settled over my life. Champ seemed to be handing me the leash, urging, *"Come on, Momma! Let's fetch some happiness!"* I began to understand that the power of love and acceptance could transform lives—both human and canine.

Champ's unwavering spirit and deep love showed me that true change starts from within. However, channeling my pain into a *purposeful mission* became a healing gift to myself. Embracing our authenticity and appreciating the uniqueness of others paves the way for a more compassionate and inclusive world.

Through this journey, I discovered my strengths and weaknesses, learning to let go of judgments and embrace the present moment.

The challenge taught me to see the world through Champ's heart—full of wonder and enthusiasm. I realized that each interaction, no matter how small, held the *pawtential* to create a ripple effect of *pawsitivity* and kindness.

This experience transformed my outlook and reinforced the bond between Champ and me. We became partners in spreading joy and bully-breed awareness, smile by smile. The challenge was more than just a social experiment; it was a testament to the healing power of compassion.

Wagging Tails and Global Smiles: The Ripple Effect

What began as a simple, heartfelt endeavor quickly transformed into a worldwide movement. Champ's infectious smile extended its magic far beyond our daily runs. His message of love and acceptance spread like wildfire thanks to social media. People from all corners of the globe began following Champ's journey, captivated by his charm and the powerful message he embodied.

Dog communities rallied behind us, sharing Champ's posts and spreading the word. Seven leading dog magazines picked up our story and reposted it, turning Champ into an overnight superstar. His smile became a symbol of hope, breaking down barriers of fear and prejudice.

The 'tails' that came pouring in were nothing short of amazing. Inspired by Champ's posts during the *Smile Challenge,* one woman found the courage to start volunteering at her local animal shelter, something she had always wanted to do but had been too anxious to try. Then, there was an elderly man who shared that seeing Champ's smile was the highlight of his day, motivating him to go for his daily walks.

Another memorable story featured a young girl who had always been terrified of dogs because of the negative stereotypes she'd grown up with. When she met Champ, her fear melted away, replaced by admiration for his gentle nature. She even started advocating for bully breeds at her school, showing everyone that a wagging tail could be more powerful than a growl.

We also met a woman who had recently lost her dog and was deep in grief. When she saw Champ's beaming face, it brought back memories of her beloved companion, but instead of sadness, it brought comfort. She told us that Champ's smile reminded her of the love she shared with her dog and helped her start healing.

Each smile Champ inspired was changing *pawceptions* and spreading joy. His influence grew with each passing day, proving that a single act of kindness could ripple out and touch countless lives. Seeing him in action felt like watching a wagging tail sweep away the cobwebs of misunderstanding and fear.

The *100-Day Smile Challenge* was more than a challenge; it was a testament to the power of love and the resilience of the human (and canine) spirit. Champ's smile reminded us that we all have the power to make a difference, spread joy, and challenge the stereotypes that divide us.

Pawsitive Testimonials: 'Tails' of Impact

The *100-Day Smile Challenge* brought immense joy to many, and the heartfelt testimonials we received truly reflect the impact Champ had. Here are just a few examples of the inspiring messages from those touched by Champ's infectious smile and spirit:

- **Sarah Nabbs from the UK:** "Following the *100-day Challenge* brightened up my days. Dr. Harmony and Champ had a huge impact on my life, especially when I lost my dog last year. My rescue Staffy crossbreed wore the peace collar they promoted with pride. Dr. Harmony and Champ were great supporters during that tough time."

- **Alexandra from the UK:** "I first came across Champ of Avalon on Facebook. He was at the forefront of a campaign to help the world understand bully breeds. Thanks to Champ's mum, he became much more than just a dog—he led global recognition of the joy of owning bull breeds."

- **Angel Ruger, the Staffie from Down Under:** "Keep on with your amazing work for *Global Paws for Peace* via your Facebook page. Lots of love and high-paws always, your BFF Angel Ruger, the Staffie from Down Under. I happily watch over you and see that your book is coming along bully great."

These testimonials showcase the wide-reaching impact of Champ's smile and mission. Each message highlights the joy and understanding Champ brought into people's lives, emphasizing the importance of his *pawpose* to be an advocate for change.

With the success of the *100-Day Smile Challenge,* it became clear that Champ's mission was far from over. His smile had become his logo, inspiring people worldwide to live their best lives.

Barking Up the Right Tree: Champ's Role in Advocacy

As Champ's smile continued to light up the world, we realized our mission needed to grow beyond the *100-Day Smile Challenge*. Inspired by Champ's incredible impact on breaking stereotypes and spreading joy, we launched *Global Paws For Peace*. Our goal? To promote unity among all breeds and educate on breed discrimination with the same love and acceptance Champ embodied daily.

Global Paws For Peace was founded to educate, advocate, and create *pawsitive* change. Here's how we expanded our mission:

- **Educational Initiatives:** We launched programs to educate people about the misconceptions surrounding bully breeds. By sharing facts and heartwarming stories, we aimed to show that every dog deserves love and respect. Imagine Champ in spirit, wagging his tail from the great beyond, reminding us, *"Don't judge a book by its cover. We all have hearts of gold!"*

- **Community Outreach:** Our outreach programs were designed to connect directly with people, spreading our message of unity and acceptance. One notable event was the *Bully Breed Freedom Walk at Legacy Park in Cottleville, Missouri.* These events allowed people to meet and interact with bully breeds, breaking down fears and prejudices. Though Champ is no longer with us physically, his spirit continues to inspire countless hearts to open up. Picture his legacy declaring, *"See? We're just big ol' teddy bears!"*

- **Advocacy Efforts:** We partnered with other organizations to amplify our voices and advocate for peace instead of waging war against breed-specific legislation (BSL). These laws unfairly target breeds like Champ's, perpetuating myths and discrimination. By promoting unity, education, and empathy, we aim to influence policy changes and foster fair treatment for all dogs. Champ's enduring spirit is like having a furry guardian angel guiding us to show the world what true love and understanding look like.

Champ attended numerous events, winning hearts and changing minds with his charisma and gentle nature. We continue to carry Champ's spirit, ensuring his legacy of love and acceptance lives on.

Through *Global Paws For Peace,* we strive to create a world where all dogs, especially bully breeds, are treated with kindness and respect. Our mission is to empower humans to enrich the lives of these dogs, breaking down barriers and fostering understanding. Champ's legacy lives on through this advocacy work, reminding us that we can create a more compassionate and inclusive world for humans and our four-legged friends with love and determination.

As we move forward, you'll learn about our future projects and initiatives, and we invite you to keep Champ's legacy of love and freedom alive.

Are you ready to hear about these exciting plans and how we're making a difference?

Let's jump in!

Global Paws For Peace: Promoting Unity and Raising Awareness

Global Paws For Peace hosts various events throughout the year, such as the Global Canine Peace Movement. In this event, dogs wear Peace Collars to promote unity and honor Lennox the Pitbull. Additionally, we support rescue missions, education programs, and community projects.

To get involved, you can participate in the following ways:

The Peace Collar

Global Paws For Peace was founded to raise awareness about breed-specific prejudice and promote peace and unity. We started the *Global Canine Peace Movement,* symbolized by the Peace Collar, encouraging dogs worldwide to join in spreading this message. Proceeds from Peace

Collar sales support our mission, funding programs like Canine Epilepsy, New Leash On Life Rescue, and Castles 4 Canines.

Visit ThePeaceCollar.org or scan the QR code below to learn more and purchase your Peace Collar:

Visit Our Website

To get involved further, visit our website and follow us on social media for updates on events and volunteer opportunities. Your help can spread our message of love and unity even further.

Visit GlobalPawsForPeace.org or scan the QR code below:

Champ The Human Whisperer Book

If you've been inspired by the message in this book, consider paying it forward. A portion of the proceeds from *Champ The Human Whisperer* go directly to support our mission and causes. You can also gift a copy, knowing your contribution helps further Champ's legacy. Additionally, if your organization becomes an affiliate and promotes the digital version of the book, a portion of those sales will be donated directly to your organization, allowing you to support your cause and our shared mission.

The book is available on Amazon, and a portion of all proceeds supports our organization. You can also purchase the digital version directly from our website, with proceeds from both options helping to fund our mission.

If you're interested in becoming an affiliate and having a portion of the proceeds benefit your organization, please email us at info@GlobalPawsForPeace.org for more details.

Scan the QR code below to learn more about sharing or becoming an affiliate:

Pawsitive Projects Ahead

Champ's Treats: P'Mutt Butter Squirrels

Champ's Treats, a labor of love inspired by Champ's favorite things—peanut butter and chasing squirrels, quickly gained popularity when we first produced and sold them at events. They became a beloved symbol of joy and support, with organizations even asking Champ to be the mascot for their fundraisers.

Champ's Treats, especially the P'Mutt Butter Squirrels, are a unique offering in the market. We first introduced these treats at events, where they quickly gained popularity. Organizations were so impressed that they requested Champ as their mascot for fundraisers, which led to the creation of these beloved treats.

To take this idea to the next level, we aim to partner with a major supplier to bring these unique treats into major pet stores. Champ will continue to be the mascot, spreading love and joy through these tasty treats. A portion of the proceeds will support rescue organizations and other dog-related causes, ensuring that Champ's legacy continues to make a *pawsitive* impact.

A portion of the proceeds from every sale will go directly to support rescue organizations and other causes dedicated to improving the lives of dogs, especially bully breeds. Additionally, these treats can be wholesaled to different organizations, giving them a unique way to raise funds and further their missions.

Stay tuned for more updates on how you can get your paws on Champ's Treats and contribute to a greater cause!

Champ The Human Whisperer Children's Series

We plan to create a children's book series called *Champ The Human Whisperer*. Each book will focus on one of *Champ's 8 Timeless Tricks* to Be Dog-gone Happy on *Pawpose,* which I'll share in the next section of this book.

Cartoon Series

There's also a vision for a *Champ The Human Whisperer* cartoon series. Champ will teach kids about living a happy and *pawposeful* life in this show. Each episode will focus on one of Champ's tricks, helping kids learn valuable lessons through fun adventures.

Kids Card Deck

We're developing a *Champ The Human Whisperer,* Kids' Card Deck. This deck will help children learn to master the *8 Timeless Tricks* and balance their energy. It will include tips and techniques for living a conscious and fulfilling life.

Stay Connected with Champ's Mission!

Join Champ's Facebook page to stay updated on his legacy. Here, you can find updates, share heartwarming stories, and join a community that promotes happiness and unity.

Visit and like his page, Champ Bully About Town, or scan the QR code below:

As we move forward with these plans to keep Champ's legacy alive, it's important to note that not all of these ideas are entirely in motion yet—they represent the vision we're working towards. Stay tuned for more information on all the upcoming offerings, projects, and ways to get involved in spreading Champ's mission of happiness, love, and unity.

Your support and involvement can make a significant impact. Whether through spreading the word to friends, family, and your social networks or by sharing your unique contributions, every effort helps to further our mission of compassion and understanding. Your ideas and resources are not just welcome; they are essential to help expand our reach and accomplish these goals.

Champ's ultimate joy was seeing people smile, and by sharing your smile and support, you can help brighten someone's day and continue Champ's legacy of happiness and unity. Together, we can create a world filled with love, understanding, and compassion by sharing and building upon Champ's legacy.

Reflecting on Champ's Mission: A Legacy of Love and Unity

As paws and reflect on our journey with Champ, it's clear that his mission was simple yet powerful: to spread love, acceptance, and unity, one wag at a time. His smile and joy have touched countless lives from the beginning, showing that even the smallest gestures can create significant change.

Through the *100-Day Smile Challenge,* we experienced firsthand how a simple smile can break down barriers and change perceptions. Champ taught us that *love* and *acceptance* can transform us and the world around us. Despite the stereotypes and judgments he faced, Champ consistently rose above them with a wagging tail and a heart full of kindness.

Organizations like *Global Paws For Peace* are committed to carrying Champ's legacy forward, uniting all breeds in a mission of compassion and understanding. Champ has proven that bully breeds are more than their reputation—they are loving, loyal, and full of life. His journey reminds us of the importance of love, acceptance, and a little determination to make a lasting impact.

In the following chapters, we'll explore *Champ's 8 Timeless Tricks to Be Dog-gone Happy on Pawpose,* focusing on each core principle he lived by. These tricks aren't just for dogs—they're for anyone seeking a joyful life. So, grab your leash and get ready to learn how to *Bark Out Loud, Sniff it Out,* and more!

But first, Champ has a special message for you. Let's see what our furry friend has to share before we jump into the first trick: *Burying Your Bones by Letting Go.*

PART TWO

UNLEASHING CANINE WISDOM: 8 TIMELESS TRICKS FOR YOUR BEST SELF

WOOF AND WELCOME TO THE 8 TIMELESS TRICKS FROM CHAMP'S WISDOM

Hey There, Pawsome Friend!

It's *Champ Avalon* here, your furry guide and loyal buddy. I hope you're wagging along with this book so far!

Now, it's time to shift gears and dive into the tricks that shaped my journey. Get ready to wag your tail, perk up those ears, and soak in some wisdom from man's best friend!

As we venture into this next phase of our adventure, I invite you to keep an open mind, a willing heart, and a ready spirit. High paw for taking the time to work on yourself—you're on the right path, and I'm here to guide you every step of the way!

Each trick starts with story time, where Momma shares how I helped her master the trick and the lessons she learned along the way. Afterward, I'll share my woof wisdom and give you tips on how to master the trick yourself. The first trick starts with Momma's story about burying old bones to make room for new treasures, setting the stage for the rest of the journey.

So, get ready to participate, stay engaged, and have some tail-wagging fun as we emBARK on this journey together.

Are you ready?

Let's sniff out some happiness and make your life as joyful as a long walk in the park!

Woofs and wags,
Champ Avalon 🐾

CHAPTER 08

TRICK #1 – BURY YOUR BONES BY LETTING GO

Have you ever watched a dog bury a bone? It's like they're on a top-secret mission! Dogs have a natural instinct to hide their treasures, and there's a lot we can learn from it. When Champ buried his bones, it wasn't just about hiding them—it was about the anticipation of finding them again later. He would dig with such focus and determination, then carefully cover his bone, knowing that rediscovery would bring renewed joy.

This behavior got me thinking: *why do dogs bury their bones, and what can we learn from it?* Dogs instinctively understand that sometimes you must let go of something now to enjoy it even more later. They bury their bones but never forget about them, savoring the joy of unearthing them when the time is right.

This idea of burying and rediscovering can teach us a lot about life. Just like Champ eagerly dug up his bones, we can uncover hidden treasures within ourselves by letting go of fears, doubts, and outdated beliefs. It's an ongoing process—releasing what holds us back to discover new joys.

In this chapter, we'll dive into this instinct and how it applies to our lives. With Champ as our guide, we'll learn how letting go of fears, insecurities, and limiting beliefs can lead us to uncover new joys and deeper parts of our true selves. So, grab your shovel (or your paws), and let's start digging!

Story Time with Champ: How Momma Dug Deep & Buried Her Bones

As mentioned, I often felt judged for even the smallest things as a kid. Growing up in a family with strong religious convictions meant following many rules: no makeup, no jewelry, and no TV on Friday nights. Everyone seemed to have opinions about right and wrong, and I was always on the wrong side. This constant judgment made me highly critical of myself, striving for *pawfection* in everything I did, hoping to be accepted.

Years later, when tragedy struck our family, I remember my uncle's sudden death vividly. He always talked about his dreams—taking a vacation, building his dream house, finding someone special. But he never got to do any of it. That hit me hard. I realized I was living the same way; I was always planning but never really living. It was a wake-up call, but my inner battles didn't just disappear.

I became a classic *Type A* personality—always busy, consistently achieving. I graduated from chiropractic school with honors, built a successful business, and drove a great car. On the outside, I had it all. But inside, I was exhausted and unhappy. It felt like there was a dark hole inside me that nothing could fill.

Then came the real turning point. I went through a divorce and a failed business partnership that cost me everything I'd built. I started a new business with a new life partner, which also ended in heartbreak and financial loss. It felt like I was constantly picking up the pieces, running two companies, and barely keeping my head above water.

Just when I thought things couldn't get worse, I was diagnosed with *uterine cancer.* That's when I truly understood what it meant to let go. I had been trying to control everything in my life, but cancer showed me that I needed to surrender. I had to let go of my fears and need for control and be vulnerable.

During this challenging time, Champ came into my life. He taught me to see life with my heart, not just my eyes. His struggles as a bully breed, constantly judged for his appearance, mirrored my own experiences of feeling judged and misunderstood. Together, we learned to let go of our past and embrace the present.

So, here I am, just over four weeks after surgery, feeling a sense of peace I never thought *pawssible*. I've found new treasures in life by letting go and burying my bones—my fears, doubts, and need for control. I know there will be more challenges ahead, but with Champ's lessons, I'm ready to face them. It's all about burying those bones and getting excited about what we'll find when we open up to new *pawssibilities*.

Uncovering New Treasures: Lighten Your Load

Letting go has been a huge part of my journey, and it all started with some major life changes. First, I moved out of a house I had lived in for seventeen years. Then, I sold almost everything I owned, about 95% of it, and ended a long-term relationship. Together, we even sold the business we had built. Talk about burying some serious bones! It was tough, but making space for new beginnings was necessary.

Just when I thought I had everything figured out, I received the diagnosis that turned my world upside down—uterine cancer. *Seriously?* I had always been the one to fix things, to handle whatever life threw my way. But this time, it wasn't about finding a solution but facing the unknown and surrendering to the journey ahead. I had to rely on faith and inner strength like never before.

The decision to undergo surgery and let go of my uterus was one of the most challenging choices I've ever made. The thought of surgery scared me more than trying to heal naturally, but I knew it was the right path to take. During my four-week recovery, I discovered the empowering nature of letting go. Instead of being the doctor, I allowed myself to fully experience being the patient. Embracing the healing process, I began to feel lighter and more at peace.

Guided by Champ's wisdom, I learned the value of letting go, much like burying a bone. Releasing what no longer served me made room for new opportunities. This made me stronger and more confident in facing challenges. Like Champ, I've discovered that the best prizes are found when we let go of the old and make space for the new.

So, whether you're moving to a new place, downsizing, ending relationships, or facing health scares, remember that letting go is the key to uncovering life's hidden treasures. With each 'bone' you bury, you lighten your load and find the strength to keep going. Guided by Champ's lessons, you'll be ready to tackle any challenge that comes your way.

Buddy's Story: Drop the Rock, Lighten Your Load

Let me tell you a *tail-wagging story,* one that's not just for humans but for dogs as well. It's about a young pup named Buddy who learned a big lesson about letting go.

Buddy played fetch with his friends at the park one sunny afternoon. He loved chasing after sticks and balls, but today, he found a special rock he had to carry everywhere. Buddy held onto that rock like it was the most precious treasure in the world. He ran around, showing it off to all his friends, but the rock soon felt heavy.

As the day went on, Buddy noticed something strange. The more he held onto the rock, the harder it was to play and run around. His paws got tired, and his mouth ached from gripping it tightly. His friends, busy chasing their toys and enjoying the park, saw Buddy struggling and barked, *"Drop the rock, Buddy! Drop the rock!"*

But Buddy was stubborn. He thought that holding onto the rock made him special. He didn't want to let it go, even though it made him miserable. Finally, Buddy's best friend, Max, came over and nudged him gently. *"Buddy, sometimes you must let go of something to enjoy everything else. Just drop the rock."*

Buddy looked at Max, then at the rock. It was heavy and covered in slobber, not as special as he first thought. Buddy took a deep breath, opened his mouth, and let the rock fall to the ground. Instantly, he felt lighter, free. He wagged his tail and ran around, feeling the wind in his fur. Buddy realized Max was right—letting go of the rock made him feel much better.

The moral of Buddy's story is simple: sometimes, we hold onto things that weigh us down, thinking they're important. But letting go can lighten our load and find more joy in life. Just like Buddy discovered that dropping the rock made him happier, we can find happiness by releasing what no longer serves us.

So next time you're feeling weighed down, remember Buddy's story. *Drop the rock, lighten your load, and uncover the treasures life has waiting for you.* After all, life is much more fun when you're running free with your tail wagging!

Champ's Trick #1 in Action: Practical Steps to Bury Your Bones

Pawsitive Practices to Unleash the Wisdom: Alright, pups and pals, it's time to put Champ's wisdom into action! Here are some tail-wagging practical tips to help you lighten your load and bury your bones:

- **Brush It Off—Letting Go of Resistance and Negative Thinking:** Just like Champ was able to shake off whatever bothered him, you can let go of resistance and negative thinking. If something doesn't go your way, take a deep breath, shake it off, and move on to the next adventure. Embrace life as it comes and stay pawsitive. *After all, why bark at the wind when you can chase a squirrel instead?*

- **Puppy Eyes and Forgiveness—Finding Innocence in Others and Yourself:** Champ's ability to see the good in everyone and forgive easily was a lesson. He forgave even when someone stepped on his tail or forgot his snack. Learning to find innocence in others and yourself is key. Forgive others and yourself to find peace and move forward with a lighter heart. If Champ could forgive the mailman for skipping his daily treat, surely, you could forgive yourself for your mistakes.

- **Shake Off the Mud—Releasing the Past and Reclaiming Inner Power:** Dogs live in the moment, and Champ was no exception. He didn't dwell on the past, and neither should you. Release old hurts and regrets to reclaim your inner power. You can move forward with a wagging tail by letting go of the past, just like Champ shook off the mud after a romp in the rain.

- **New Parks, New Adventures—Embracing Change to Free the Soul:** Champ was always ready for a new adventure and didn't fear change. Embrace change with open paws, whether moving to a new place or starting a new chapter in life. Embracing change can lead to growth and deeper happiness. If Champ could get excited about a new park, you can enjoy new opportunities.

- **Lighten Your Load—Finding Inner Peace by Letting Go:** Champ's most important lesson is the value of lightening your load. Let go of what no longer serves you—physical *pawssessions,* old habits, or negative emotions. This will bring a sense of inner peace. Life is too short to carry unnecessary burdens. Lighten your load and find joy in the simple things, just like running freely with your ears flapping in the wind.

Woof Wisdom: Champ's Art of Letting Go

"Woof woof, friend! It's time to practice burying your bones and letting go. Like I would dig and hide my treasures, you can release what's weighing you down. Remember, it's not about holding on but finding joy in letting go. I'm here, wagging my tail, cheering you on every step of the way!"

Wrapping Up Trick #1: Bury Your Bones and Let Go

As we wrap up Trick #1, let's *paws* and reflect on all the tail-wagging *wisdom* we've uncovered with Champ. By practicing the art of letting go, we've learned to lighten our load, imagining ourselves *burying those heavy bones* and experiencing the freedom that comes with it. Life is about finding joy in the little things, those small moments that often go unnoticed, and not letting past burdens weigh us down.

Embracing the journey of *self-discovery* and *inner peace,* we realized that, like Champ, who was always eager to dig up new treasures, we, too, can uncover hidden gems within ourselves. Each step we take towards *letting go* brings us closer to a lighter, happier life.

Champ's wisdom guides us through challenges, showing us how to uncover life's treasures with a wagging tail, a forgiving heart, and an adventurous spirit. Following his example, we can navigate *ruff times* with strength and serenity, always ready to discover the joy and peace beneath the surface.

Having learned to *bury our bones and let go,* we are ready for the next exciting adventure. It's time to live in the present with *pooch-time consciousness (PTC)!* In the next chapter, we explore Trick #2: how to fully embrace the present moment, just like Champ did with his unending enthusiasm and joyful presence. We'll dive into the world of *PTC* and discover the joy of living in the moment.

Woof woof, here we go!

CHAPTER 09

TRICK #2 – LIVING IN POOCH-TIME CONSCIOUSNESS

Have you ever watched a dog sniff the ground, wag their tail, or bask in the sunshine? Like my best buddy Champ, dogs live entirely in the present moment—a state I call pooch-time consciousness (PTC). This mindset keeps them joyful, peaceful, and deeply connected to the world around them. Dogs don't dwell on the past or worry about the future; instead, they embrace each moment with wonder and excitement, finding joy in the simplest things—playing fetch, greeting you at the door, or napping in a sunny spot.

As humans, we can learn a great deal from this approach. Living in PTC can bring us fulfillment and peace. When we let go of concerns about the past and future, we open ourselves to truly enjoying the beauty of life. *But how does living in the present moment translate to our daily lives?* Regularly practicing pooch-time consciousness allows us to fully embrace this concept and integrate it into our routines.

I mentioned earlier that my uncle's tragic death in a plane crash forced me to confront the importance of living a life with no regrets—a lesson that took years to understand. However, watching Champ live in the moment daily taught me the value of cherishing the present. Champ embodies peace, patience, and kindness in everything he does, and he showed me how to find joy in the here and now. My hope is to share how embracing *pooch-time consciousness* can bring the same sense of peace and joy into your life.

Living in the Moment: Story Time with Champ

Life teaches us powerful lessons in unexpected ways. One of my most significant lessons came from my beloved Champ during a simple run in the park. It was a beautiful, sunny day, and Champ and I were out for our usual afternoon run. I was preoccupied with thoughts about ending my relationship, worrying about the future, and dwelling on past mistakes. My mind was everywhere but in the present.

Meanwhile, Champ was having the time of his life. He sniffed every tree, rolled in the grass, and investigated the bushes. His enthusiasm was infectious, but I was too wrapped up in my thoughts to enjoy the moment. Then, something special happened. Champ suddenly stopped and barked excitedly at a family of ducks waddling by a small pond. His eyes sparkled with delight, and he looked up at me as if to say, *"Isn't this the best thing ever?"*

At that moment, I realized how much I was missing by not being present. Champ was fully immersed in the beauty of the moment. Inspired by Champ, I took a deep breath, let go of my worries, and focused on the present. I felt the sun's warmth, listened to the park's sounds, and watched the ducks waddle by. For the first time in a long while, I felt peace and happiness wash over me.

Champ became my mentor in embracing *pooch-time consciousness* that day. His ability to live fully in the present, without worry or regret, deeply resonated with me. Inspired by his example, I shifted my *pawspective* and saw how living in the moment could transform my life. Champ's way of being led me to practice mindfulness, meditation, and other tools that help me stay grounded in the present.

His way of living in the moment has profoundly impacted me, helping me find joy in simple, everyday moments. Through his example, I learned that living in *PTC* is a fulfilling way of life.

Champ's Trick in Action #2: "Live in PTC"

Alright, friends and furry companions, it's time to put Champ's wisdom into action! Here are some tail-wagging ideas to help you embrace *pooch-time consciousness (PTC)* and live in the present moment:

- **Take a Paws—Set Aside Reflection Time**: Just like dogs take breaks to sniff around and explore, set aside a few minutes each day to stop and reflect. Find a quiet spot (your mental fire hydrant) and give yourself time to think about your day.

- **Sniff Out the Scene—Visualization Techniques**: Visualization anchors you in the present. Close your eyes and imagine a peaceful scene that brings you joy—a beach, forest, or sunny meadow. Picture every detail: colors, sounds, smells, and textures. Think of it as your mental leash—always there when you need to *paws* and reset!

- **Breathe Like a Pup—Practice Deep Breathing**: Practice deep breathing to shift your focus to the present moment. Try the 4-7-8 technique: inhale deeply through your nose for a count of four, hold your breath for seven, and exhale completely through your mouth for a count of eight. It's like taking a big whiff of your favorite treat—instantly grounding and delightful!

- **Wagging Affirmations—Use Pawsitive Affirmations**: *Pawsitive* affirmations reinforce your intention to live in the present. Choose affirmations that resonate with you, like *"I am fully present in this moment"* or *"I embrace PTC with joy and gratitude."* Repeat these affirmations daily, like your mental chew toys, to keep your thoughts happy.

Embrace *pooch-time consciousness* by incorporating *pawsitive* practices into your daily routine. Visualize peaceful scenes and use *pawsitive* affirmations to stay grounded. Like Champ, find joy in the simplest things, living with a wagging tail and a happy heart. Take a moment to *paws* and let *PTC* transform your days into a series of *tail-wagging moments!*

Woof Wisdom: Champ's Present Moment Mastery

"Woof woof, mate! It's me, Champ, here to help you live in PTC and make it pawsome! Take a few minutes each day to tune in to the moment—feel the breeze, the sun's warmth, and the ground beneath your paws, just like I do on our walks. Breathe deeply, think something pawsitive, and savor the here and now. Life's richer and more fun when you're fully engaged. Stop to sniff the roses (or whatever catches your nose), and you'll feel more connected and joyful. Go on and give it a try—I'm wagging my tail for you!"

Wrapping Up Trick #2: Living in Pooch-Time Consciousness

Living in the present moment through pooch-time consciousness (PTC) is truly transformative. By embracing PTC, you can break free from the stresses of daily life and tap into a deeper sense of joy and peace.

Champ was my greatest teacher in this practice. He had a remarkable ability to be fully present in whatever he was doing, whether chasing a ball or simply basking in the sun. His joyful spirit and calm demeanor were constant reminders to let go of worries and appreciate the beauty of each moment. Following his example, I've learned to find happiness in the simplest pleasures and to embrace life with a heart full of gratitude.

To help you live in PTC, we've shared practical tools to bring more presence and fun into your life—think of it like having a basket of your favorite squeaky toys that keep you engaged and focused.

Start with Champ's *Trick in Action #2:* "Live in PTC." Spend a few minutes each day being fully aware of your surroundings and appreciating the little moments. It's like taking a daily sniff break—an opportunity to notice your world's sights, sounds, and smells.

Remember, living in PTC is a gift you can give yourself. Embrace it, practice it, and let the peace and joy of each moment fill your life. So, wag your tail, take a deep breath, and enjoy living in the present!

Now that we've mastered living in PTC, we must let our voices be heard. Get ready for Trick #3: *Bark Out Loud (BOL)*. Just like Champ expresses himself with joyful barks and wagging tails, we will explore how to find and use our authentic voices confidently and clearly.

It's time to let your true voice be heard!

CHAPTER 10

TRICK #3 – BARK OUT LOUD: SPEAK YOUR TRUTH

Have you ever considered how powerful your bark could be? Our furry friends have much to teach us about communication! Dogs are experts at expressing their needs and feelings without uttering a single word. *Bark Out Loud* is about finding your authentic voice and speaking your truth with confidence and kindness.

Like Champ, who had an incredible ability to convey his emotions without needing words, we too can learn to communicate from the heart. His "language" came straight from his soul, and while he knew how to bark when needed, his most profound expressions were through his body language. Whether it was a tilt of his head, a Staffie *"huff"*, or a playful nudge, Champ's feelings were always evident. He showed me that you don't need to shout to be heard; sometimes, the most powerful messages are the ones expressed quietly but with authenticity.

In this chapter, we'll explore the art of deep listening, the importance of speaking from the heart, and how to express our feelings honestly. Champ will guide us in understanding the difference between passive, aggressive, and assertive communication, helping us find our inner voice and share it confidently. So, let's dive in and learn how to express ourselves fully and authentically—just like our canine companions!

Barking Your Truth: Story Time with Champ

One quiet Sunday afternoon after a long, tiring week, I was ready to relax on the couch with a book. But Champ had other plans.

As I settled in, Champ flopped down beside me with a big *sigh,* turning his head away while sneaking peeks at me from the corner of his eye. His loud *huff* made it clear he wasn't happy I wasn't giving him attention. Without barking or whining, he effectively communicated exactly how he felt.

Intrigued, I put down my book and watched Champ continue his performance, let out another exaggerated *sigh,* and looked at me directly with eyes full of expectation. His body language spoke volumes—he was saying, *"Hey, Momma, I'm here, and I need some love!"*

This moment was a powerful reminder of how much we can communicate without words. Champ's ability to express his feelings through his actions made me think about the importance of non-verbal communication. He taught me that sometimes, a heartfelt look or a gentle nudge can convey more than words ever could.

Watching Champ made me more aware of how I communicate. His *huffs* and *sighs* inspired me to pay closer attention to the unspoken messages I send and to be fully present in my interactions with others. Champ showed me that true communication comes from the heart and that expressing our needs through non-verbal speech can be as powerful as speaking out loud.

Champ's Trick in Action #3: "Speak and Listen from the Heart"

Alright, friends and fur family, let's dig into Champ's wisdom and learn to communicate like a true Champ! Here are some *pawsome* tips to help you master the art of speaking your truth with confidence:

- **Perk Up Those Ears—Deep Listening:** Just like perking up your ears to catch every sound in the park, take a few minutes each day to practice deep listening. This not only enhances your understanding of others but also strengthens your connection with them. Focus entirely on what someone is saying, tuning in to their words, emotions, and body language. This kind of listening isn't just about hearing—it's about understanding. It's the difference between a passive listener and an active one. Really engage, like when you're watching for that squirrel's every move!

- **Bark Your Truth—Honest Expression:** Practice expressing your feelings honestly and kindly. Speaking your truth is not just about communicating your needs; it's about empowerment. Start with small statements and gradually build up to more significant truths. Think of it as learning a new trick—start with the basics and work your way up to the more impressive moves. Honest expression is assertive communication. It's about saying what you feel without being aggressive or passive, like a dog standing tall and proud, barking with purpose, not just noise. Be genuine, like a dog rolling over for belly rubs.

- **Howl from the Heart—Use "I" Statements:** Use 'I' statements to express your feelings and avoid blaming or criticizing others. Speaking from your heart allows you to build and maintain healthy relationships. It's like saying, 'I need a walk,' instead of, 'You never take me out!' This keeps communication clear, focused, and non-confrontational. This approach is a great example of assertive communication—being direct and honest while respecting others' feelings. It's the key to keeping things upbeat and getting your point across without causing a ruckus.

- **Wag with Intention—Understanding Passive, Aggressive, and Assertive Communication:** Let's get a handle on the difference between passive, aggressive, and assertive communication. Imagine a dog that needs to go outside but sits silently by the door, hoping someone will notice—that's passive. Now, think of a dog barking non-stop, demanding to be let out— totally aggressive. But a dog that gently paws at the door or brings you the leash? That's assertive! It's about getting your needs met without being pushy or withdrawn. Practice this by observing your own communication patterns and adjusting them to be more like that gentle paw tap—effective and considerate.

Using these tips, you'll bark your truth and listen deeply and confidently to express yourself. Whether you're perking up your ears to listen or barking your truth, let Champ's wisdom guide you in mastering the art of communication. Let's wag those tails and speak from the heart!

Woof Wisdom: Champ's Voice of Truth

"Woof woof, friend! It's time to practice speaking up and being yourself. Just like I used my huffs and body language to show Momma how I felt, you can use your actions to share your feelings and thoughts. Start by really listening to others with your heart—pay attention to what they're saying. When it's your turn to talk, speak honestly and clearly. It's not about being the loudest but about being genuine. Go ahead and give it a try—I am wagging my tail and rooting for you!"

Wrapping Up Trick #3: Bark Out Loud

Let's recap the tail-wagging wisdom Champ has shared with us. We've explored the importance of expressing yourself honestly and listening deeply. Like Champ communicated his feelings through a wagging tail or a gentle nudge, you can let your true emotions shine.

Champ taught us that genuine communication goes beyond words; it comes from the heart. By learning to *Bark Out Loud,* we can authentically share our deepest thoughts and feelings, just as our furry friends do. When we communicate sincerely, we strengthen our connections and experience profound joy and inspiration.

This chapter has highlighted the power of deep listening, heartfelt expression, and assertive communication without aggression. Think of a dog seeking attention—not by barking non-stop, but by bringing its favorite toy to you or resting its head on your lap. This gentle, non-verbal communication often speaks louder than words. We can take a cue from

100

this, being clear and direct in expressing our needs while avoiding passive hints or pushy demands. This kind of assertiveness, paired with the subtle power of non-verbal cues, boosts self-confidence and fosters deeper connections with others.

With *Champ's Trick in Action,* you're now equipped to put these lessons into practice. It's not about being the loudest—it's about being genuine. Embrace the challenge of speaking your truth and listening deeply. Often, listening rather than barking is the more powerful choice, allowing you to communicate authentically and enrich your relationships, leading to a more fulfilling life.

Remember to speak and listen from the heart. Champ's wisdom is here to guide you, and the world is ready to hear your unique voice. His spirit is with you every step of the way!

Now, it's time for the next adventure. The upcoming chapter will dive into Trick #4: *Love is a Four-Legged Word.* Just like our furry friends show us unconditional love, we'll explore how to give and receive love in its purest form.

Together, we'll uncover the incredible power of love in our lives!

CHAPTER 11

TRICK #4 – LOVE IS A FOUR-LEGGED WORD

Dogs have a special way of melting even the coldest hearts with their unconditional love and loyalty. This is what *Love is a Four-Legged Word* is all about. Dogs leave paw prints on our hearts, showing us what real love looks like.

Imagine seeing life through a dog's heart—where love is pure, endless, and always flowing. Dogs don't hold grudges or stay mad. They forgive quickly, live happily, and spread comfort and affection. This chapter will show how adopting a dog's view of love can change our lives. We become a source of love by learning to love ourselves first. When we show up as love, we naturally give and receive it, attracting more love into our lives, just like dogs do. This way, our relationships improve, and our lives become full of understanding and joy. We stop searching for love because we realize we already are love, and that's when we truly connect with others in the best ways.

Self-love isn't just a phrase; it's essential for our lives. When we love ourselves, we respect and care for ourselves, which helps us love others deeply and truly. With his loving nature, Champ taught me the importance of being a source of unconditional love. Now, let's learn how to use this dog-like love and bring it into every part of our lives, changing how we interact with others and how we feel inside.

Wagging Tails and Warm Hearts: Story Time with Champ

With his never-ending love and kindness, Champ has shown me what genuine compassion is all about. His caring nature helped me open my heart and let go of the grudges I used to hold.

One moment really stands out. My ex-partner (the one that took Champ) was being difficult, and I was super angry. Champ sensed it and nudged me to take him for a walk. As we walked, his happy energy was infectious. He smiled at everyone we passed, wagging his tail with pure joy.

Champ didn't hold onto negative feelings. If he was upset, he showed it and then moved on, always returning to being loving and happy. I realized that if Champ could let go so quickly, why couldn't I? It was a powerful moment.

Back home, Champ curled up beside me, resting his head on my lap. I could feel the warmth of his unconditional love. It was then I decided to let go of my grudge. I chose to see my ex-partner's behavior with compassion and used our interactions as a chance to forgive. I felt an immediate sense of relief and freedom.

Forgiving is a powerful form of self-love. We rise above the situation by choosing to forgive and show love despite someone's actions. This helps us not take things personally because we have healed our inner child wounds. *Inner child wounds* are the past hurts and traumas we experienced when we were younger. These wounds can make us feel unheard, unseen, or unimportant and block us from being open to love. When we hold onto these past hurts, they can affect how we interact with others and ourselves.

Letting go of past hurts allows us to heal and be more open to love. We can heal these inner child wounds by showing up as love, even in difficult situations. Being an example of true love helps us heal ourselves. We also learn to set boundaries and honor our needs. By standing firm with love and not allowing others to bring us down, we teach them to respect us.

Taking care of my *inner child* and practicing self-love has changed me. Champ, the *Nanny Dog,* taught me how to nurture my inner child. I've learned to treat myself with the same kindness and compassion he showed me daily. I've become more patient, forgiving, and open-hearted by embracing self-love. Forgiveness has helped me love myself more deeply, leading to more joy and better connections with others.

I've discovered that *love is a four-legged word* through Champ's example. His ability to forgive and live joyfully has taught me to do the same, leading to a life where grudges are replaced by compassion and bitterness is replaced by understanding.

Champ's Trick in Action #4: "Embrace the Four-Legged Love"

Alright, pack, it's time to put Champ's wisdom into action! Here are some tail-wagging tips to help you love unconditionally:

- **Pamper Yourself Like a Pup:** Treat yourself with kindness every day. Whether it's enjoying a small treat, doing something fun, or thinking about what makes you unique, it's like giving your soul a belly rub!

- **Bury the Grudge Bone:** Write a letter (you don't have to send it) to someone you need to forgive. Share your feelings and then let them go, like burying an old bone you don't need to dig up again. Feel the weight lift off your shoulders as you let go of that grudge.

- **Wagging Affirmations:** Create a daily affirmation that reminds you how great you are, and say it every morning. Look in the mirror and say, *"I am pawsitively amazing!"* Let these words fill your heart and boost your confidence.

- **Paws and Reflect:** Spend a few minutes each day thinking about past hurts and how they may block you from love. Ask yourself,

"Where have I felt these feelings before?" and *"What happened when I was younger that made me feel this way?"* By understanding these inner child wounds, you can gently let them go. Imagine you're training your mind to understand and accept these emotions. When you show love to yourself, you open the door to more love from others.

By embracing these *pawsitive* practices, you'll unleash the wisdom of unconditional love and compassion. Like Champ, you'll find joy in the simple things, spread love effortlessly, and make every day a tail-wagging adventure.

Woof Wisdom: Champ's Unconditional Love

"Woof woof, friend! It's time to learn the true meaning of love from a four-legged pawspective. Just like I love my Momma unconditionally, you can learn to love yourself and others with the same open heart. Take a moment each day to show yourself some love—give yourself a treat, nap, or just wag your tail in happiness. And remember, forgiving yourself is as important as forgiving others. Write down your feelings, let them go, and keep your heart open. Let's spread some pawsome love together!"

Wrapping Up Trick #4: Embrace the Four-Legged Love

Let's take a moment to think about all the tail-wagging wisdom we've learned from Champ. Practicing self-love and deep compassion can transform your life like a dog expressing joy with a wagging tail.

Champ's teachings on self-love, forgiveness, and unconditional love are a beacon of hope. By acknowledging and releasing old wounds, particularly those from our inner child, we can pave the way for more love and joy. This is not about being passive or aggressive, but about showing up authentically and setting healthy boundaries. These practices have the power to heal old hurts and foster deeper, more meaningful connections.

With *Champ's Trick #4 in Action,* you're equipped to put these lessons into practice. Take the time to understand and heal from past experiences, acknowledging where these feelings originate and how they impact you today. Embrace the concept that *you are love,* and when you show love to yourself, you invite more love from others. It's all about opening your heart. When you do, your relationships flourish, and you experience a profound sense of peace.

So, embrace the *four-legged love* and let it guide you to a life of happiness and freedom. The world is waiting to see your unique glow, and we're celebrating your journey with you.

Now, let's get ready for the next exciting adventure. The upcoming chapter will dive into Trick #5: *Sniff it Out—Trust Your Instincts.* Like our furry friends use their noses to navigate the world, we'll explore how to trust our instincts and follow our true path. So, let's trot on over and discover the power of trusting your gut!

CHAPTER 12

TRICK #5 – SNIFF IT OUT: TRUST YOUR INSTINCTS

Follow the Nose! It Always Knows! Have you ever watched a dog, nose to the ground, fully absorbed in following a scent trail? Dogs trust their instincts, letting their noses lead them to hidden treasures. We humans could learn a lot from this natural ability. Too often, we doubt ourselves, let fear influence our choices, and struggle to follow our inner guide.

In *Sniff it Out: Trust Your Instincts,* we explore the power of intuition. Like Champ, who never second-guesses his nose, we can learn to trust our inner compass to guide us toward what's best for us. By embracing this instinctual wisdom, we can make decisions with confidence and clarity.

Get ready to dive into *Trick #5* and discover the power of following your instincts!

Sniffing Out Wisdom: Story Time with Champ

Watching Champ sniff out rabbits in the yard has taught me profound lessons about trusting my instincts. One day, I observed him methodically following a scent trail, nose to the ground, fully immersed in his task. No rabbits were in sight, but that didn't discourage him. *Champ trusted his nose,* knowing the scent would eventually lead him to his goal.

This simple act of trust and determination struck a chord with me. Like Champ, I needed to learn to trust my instincts without questioning every detail or letting fear cloud my decision.

I remember a specific instance when I had to decide about a business opportunity. My initial reaction was fear-based; I worried about the *pawtential* risks and what could go wrong. However, as I watched Champ confidently sniffing out his unseen prey, I felt a shift. I decided to step back, quiet my mind, and listen to my inner guide.

In that moment of stillness, I distinguished between my fear and intuition. My intuition told me this opportunity aligned with my values and goals, even though it felt risky. *Trusting my instincts,* I moved forward confidently, and it was one of the best decisions I've ever made.

This lesson from Champ has been invaluable. By trusting my instincts, I've made choices that align with my highest good, leading to more fulfilling and authentic experiences in my life. Champ's unwavering trust in his nose has taught me to believe in my inner guide, knowing it will lead me where I need to go.

Champ's Trick in Action #5: "Follow Your Nose to Wisdom"

Alright, friends and furballs, it's time to put Champ's wisdom into action! Here are some tail-wagging suggestions to help you sniff it out and trust your instincts:

- **Sniff Out Your Inner Guide Daily**: Take a few moments daily to check in with your instincts. When faced with a decision, *paws* and listen to your inner guide. It's like sniffing the breeze and getting your bearings before running off on a new adventure.

- **Meditate Like a Mutt**: Practice mindfulness techniques such as meditation, breathing exercises, or visualization to enhance your connection to intuition. Picture yourself in a calm, serene place— maybe a sunny spot in the yard where you can relax and let your mind settle.

- **Journal Your Nose-ventures**: Keep a journal to record your intuitive feelings and the outcomes of trusting them. Reflect on how your intuition has guided you. Think of it as documenting all the exciting scents you've picked up and where they've led you.

By incorporating these practices into your daily routine, you can strengthen your intuition and become more attuned to your inner guide. This will help you make better choices, stay true to yourself, and navigate life's challenges with the confidence of a dog following its nose. Trust your instincts and let your inner wisdom lead the way!

Woof Wisdom: Champ's Intuitive Insights

"Woof woof, friend! It's time to sniff out the truth and trust your instincts, just like I do when I follow the scent of squirrels that have scampered across the fence. Your nose knows best, so listen to your inner GPS. Take a moment each day to tune in and follow your inner nose. Keep track of how it helps you make the best choices. With practice, you will trust your inner wisdom and wag your tail confidently!"

Wrapping Up Trick #5: Sniff it Out - Trust Your Instincts

We've learned how simple it is to trust ourselves and how powerful it can be when we do. Trusting your instincts is like a dog sniffing out a new scent—it helps you make the best decisions. Champ showed us that we can find the right path in life by following our gut feelings.

This trick teaches us to listen to our inner voice, understand the difference between fear and intuition, and use tools to strengthen our instincts. These skills help us make better choices and connect more deeply with others.

With *Champ's Trick in Action,* you have practical steps to practice these lessons. It's not about following every whim but about trusting your direction. As you do this, you'll make better decisions, have stronger friendships, and feel more confident.

So, believe in yourself and let your inner voice lead the way. We're here, celebrating every step you take on this incredible journey!

Now, get ready for the next adventure. The upcoming chapter digs into Trick #6: *Become Your Own Best Friend.* Just as dogs are loyal and loving, we'll learn how to build a strong, caring relationship with ourselves. Let's go unleash the power of self-friendship!

CHAPTER 13

TRICK #6 – BECOME YOUR OWN BEST FRIEND

Whoever said diamonds are a girl's best friend never had a Champ! In the world of wagging tails and endless devotion, dogs show us a profound truth: we are worthy of becoming our best friends. *Dogs are masters at being best friends, teaching us through their actions how we should treat ourselves.*

Imagine getting mail marked "Royal Mail" with Queen Elizabeth II's silhouette, addressed to your beloved *Sir Avalon.* That's how Champ lived—like royalty, reminding me that we, too, deserve to feel special. In this chapter, we dive into *becoming our own best friend* and feeling worthy. We'll learn from our loyal canine companions how to practice self-care and treat ourselves with the same kindness and commitment they show us.

Get ready to *unleash* the secret to complete self-care and sharing your light. By viewing ourselves as our dogs see us, we can recognize the good within us, helping us live our best lives. With Champ's wisdom, we'll learn to be gentle, kind, and appreciative of ourselves. Embrace this *pawspective* to discover how to live happily and fulfill your *pawtential,* striving to become the person our dogs believe us to be.

Treating Yourself Like Royalty: Story Time with Champ

Living with Champ was like a lesson in kindness, dedication, and self-care. From the start, Champ's royal treatment showed me how I should treat myself.

One day, a package from England with "Royal Mail" stamped on it came addressed to Champ. Inside were treats from his fur-friend Mia, who followed his adventures from far away. The package had Queen Elizabeth II's silhouette on it, making me realize Champ was getting first-class treatment, and he knew he deserved it.

Watching Champ enjoy his royal status, I realized I needed to treat myself with the same care and consideration. Champ always got his meals on time, claimed the best spot on the couch, and enjoyed long walks or runs every day. He expected the best, making me think about how often I ignored my needs.

Champ had a funny habit of lying on the stairs and staring at himself in the mirror as if to say, *"I am worthy."* This daily ritual showed his confidence and made me realize I should see myself similarly.

One of the biggest self-care lessons came from Champ's nap times. He had no problem curling up for a midday snooze, reminding me that rest is essential. I never used to nap, but now I let myself rest when needed, understanding that rest is necessary, not a reward.

I learned to set loving boundaries through Champ's example without feeling guilty. Just as Champ would assert himself when he needed space or attention, I began to voice my needs clearly and confidently. This helped me become my own best friend, treating myself with the same love and respect I deserve to receive from others. When we treat ourselves the way we want to be treated, we teach others to show up for us, too.

Even though Champ has crossed the *rainbow bridge,* his influence has changed how I approach self-care and self-love. By remembering his behavior and mirroring his actions, I've learned to cherish myself. Going forward, I will walk this journey as my best friend, always carrying his lessons with me.

Champ's Trick in Action #6: "Pamper Yourself Like Royalty"

Alright, peeps, let's get ready to embrace Champ's wisdom! Here are some *pawsome* tips to help you become your own best friend:

Tip #1: Daily Pampering Rituals

- *Fetch Your Happy Place:* Take time each day to practice self-care. This can be as simple as walking, reading a good book, or indulging in a favorite hobby. Think of it as fetching moments of joy throughout your day.

- *Royal Spa Time:* Treat yourself to a soothing bath with your favorite bath salts or oils. Light some candles, play relaxing music, and turn your bathroom into a personal spa. (Let me be clear, bath time was not relaxing for Champ. However, when I used to relax in the bath, he would be right by the tub relaxing with me.)

Tip #2: Set Loving Boundaries

- *Bark Your Limits:* Practice loving boundaries by saying no to tasks or requests that drain your energy. It's okay to protect your peace and prioritize your well-being.

- *Guard Your Yard:* Imagine your energy as a beautiful yard. Just as you wouldn't let anyone trample on it, don't let tasks or people overstep your boundaries. Be firm yet kind in communicating your limits.

Tip #3: Joyful Activities

- *Wag-Worthy Fun:* Make a list of activities that bring you joy and incorporate them into your daily routine. Whether playing fetch (or a human equivalent), gardening, or painting, ensure you have time for fun.

- *Pawsome Adventures:* Plan regular adventures that excite you. It could be a weekend hike, a trip to a new city, or simply exploring a new *pawsuit*. Keep your life vibrant and full of experiences that make you wag your tail.

Tip #4: Delegate and Ask for Help

- *Pass the Bone:* Delegate tasks you can't handle on your own and be open to receiving help from others. There's no shame in sharing the load.

- *Teamwork Treats:* Encourage a culture of teamwork at home and work. Remember, even Champ knew when to let his fur friends pitch in. It's okay to rely on your pack for support.

Tip #5: Embrace Self-Compassion

- *Treat Yourself with a Gentle Paw:* When you make a mistake, treat yourself with the same kindness you would offer a friend. Be quick to forgive and move forward without dwelling on past errors.

- *Love Yourself Fur-real:* Regularly remind yourself that you deserve love and kindness. Practice self-compassion by acknowledging your efforts and celebrating your achievements, no matter how small.

Taking care of yourself can change your life. Be kind, honest, and forgiving to yourself. Set boundaries and let go of guilt. By doing this, you can become your own best friend, just like Champ has taught me. So, let's wag our tails, practice self-care, and live our best lives, one *paw* step at a time!

Woof Wisdom: Champ's Self-Care Secrets

"Woof woof, friends! It's time to pamper yourselves like the royalty you are. Take a moment each day to do something special just for you. It could be a pleasant stroll, planning a getaway, or enjoying your favorite meal. Set those loving boundaries, and don't be afraid to ask for help.

Remember, you deserve to be treated like the precious diamond you are. Let's shine together and wag our tails in self-love and joy!"

Wrapping Up Trick #6: Becoming Your Own Best Friend

Let's reflect on the tail-wagging wisdom we've gathered from Champ. Taking care of yourself and becoming your best friend means looking after your mind, body, heart, and soul.

It's not just about treating yourself to nice things. It's about being kind to yourself, setting boundaries, and accepting who you are. Champ has shown me how important it is to care for myself with empathy and tenderness. You can do the same by practicing self-care daily and setting healthy limits.

Through my journey with Champ, I've learned to be gentle with myself, establish boundaries without feeling bad, and realize that asking for help is a sign of strength. These practices have changed my life and helped me become my best friend. Remember, you are *worthy* of putting yourself first and treating yourself with the same love and respect you give to others.

Now it's your turn. Use this chapter's tools and insights to start your self-care and self-respect journey. Remember, you deserve to be treated like royalty. Follow Champ's tips, practice self-care daily, and celebrate your worth. Let your inner best friend shine and transform your life.

In the next chapter, we'll dive into Trick #7: *Wag Your Tail and Have Fun Doing It!* Get ready to explore the joy of living with enthusiasm and playfulness. Let's trot on over and discover how to bring more fun into our lives!

CHAPTER 14

TRICK #7 – WAG YOUR TAIL AND HAVE FUN DOING IT!

Have you ever heard of a Staffy yodel or laugh? If not, *paws* right now and watch a YouTube video because that joy is infectious! Imagine starting each day with that kind of enthusiasm, ready to sing in the shower and embrace whatever comes your way. *Wag Your Tail and Have Fun Doing It!* is about living life with the same passion and joy our dogs bring to every moment.

Champ didn't just wag his tail; he wagged it with his heart. His joyful spirit and zest for life were contagious, inspiring us to wake up daily with excitement and a sense of adventure. Champ's boundless energy and playful nature reminded me to find joy in the little things and to approach life with a cheerful attitude. Whether chasing a ball, greeting a friend, or simply enjoying a sunny day, Champ showed me that happiness comes from within and is always worth sharing. His legacy of love and joy continues to inspire me every day.

In this chapter, we explore how to look at life through the eyes of our hearts, much like our dogs do. Learn to embrace each day fully, making the most of every moment. Discover ways to cultivate a *pawsitive* mindset, find joy in everyday activities, and, most importantly, spread happiness to those around you. By following Champ's example, you can turn ordinary moments into extraordinary experiences filled with laughter and love, not just for yourself but for everyone you touch.

Get ready to dive into the delightful world of wagging your tail and having fun! Let's discover how to live with enthusiasm, embrace life's adventures, and share our joy with others. Remember, life is a journey best enjoyed with curiosity and a playful spirit.

Wagging Through Life: Story Time with Champ

Champ's enthusiastic nature has profoundly influenced my outlook on life. One of my favorite memories is watching him greet each morning with joyfulness. He chased his ball, ran through piles of leaves, and shook his head gleefully. His infectious enthusiasm made me realize that every day is a gift, an opportunity to start fresh and experience life's wonders.

One of Champ's favorite activities was *playing laser tag.* He would chase that tiny red dot around the floor, up the walls, and even jump to the top of a door frame, trying to catch it. I remember feeling particularly overwhelmed by the pressures of work and personal commitments one morning. Sensing my mood, Champ nudged me and ran to his *laser pointer.* His eyes were full of anticipation.

Deciding to take a break, I picked up the *laser pointer* and watched as Champ instantly sprang into action. He darted around the room, his excitement growing with each leap. At one point, he managed to jump to the top of the door frame, *determined to catch that untouchable red dot.* His joy and determination were contagious, and soon, I found myself laughing and cheering him on.

That simple act of play transformed my entire day. I realized how important it was to infuse my life with moments of joy and fun, much like the way Champ did. I began incorporating more play into my daily routine—whether taking a break to dance around the living room, going for a walk in the yard, or simply enjoying a good laugh. These small but significant changes have tremendously impacted my overall well-being and outlook on life.

Champ's zest for life taught me to appreciate the little things, find joy in the mundane, and live each day enthusiastically and passionately.

Adopting his playful attitude has made my days more enjoyable and encouraged a more profound sense of gratitude and happiness in my life.

Champ's Trick in Action #7: "Play, Laugh, and Smile Like a Staffy"

Ok, *pawsome* humans, it's time to put Champ's wisdom into action! Here are some tail-wagging ideas to help you embrace life with joy and enthusiasm:

- **Sniff Out Adventure**: Get outdoors and connect with nature often. Take walks, go barefoot in the grass or sand, and rediscover the joy of play. Let yourself be curious and adventurous like a pup exploring a new park.

- **Let the Sun Shine In**: If you can't get outside, open the curtains and windows as often as possible. Let in fresh air and sunlight to brighten your day. Imagine it as letting in the world outside, much like a dog sticking its head out of a car window.

- **Smile Like a Staffy**: Practice smiling in a *Staffy* style—big, bright, and often. Let your smile reach your eyes and light up your face. Think of how Champ's smile always made everything better and try to spread that same joy.

- **Fetch Your Passion**: Stir up some passion by engaging in activities that bring you joy. Listen to your favorite music, sing at the top of your lungs, or enjoy a good joke. Find those moments that make your tail wag, and make time for them regularly.

- **Unleash Your Inner Pup**: Don't be afraid to be silly and playful. Watch cartoons, play dress-up (as I did with Champ throughout his life in all those silly seasonal costumes), and let your playful side shine.

- **Take Paws for Daydreams**: Set aside time to daydream and let your mind wander. Visualize your biggest dreams and let the excitement fuel your motivation to achieve them.

- **Chase the Simple Joys**: Like a dog exploring a new park, find happiness in the small things. Spend time drawing or painting, play your favorite game, or savor your favorite snack. Relish and celebrate these everyday pleasures.

- **Roll with the Good Times**: Embrace spontaneity. If an opportunity for fun comes up, say yes! Let yourself roll with it and enjoy the ride, whether it's an impromptu road trip or a surprise outing.

Bubbly Bliss: Learning from Champ's Joy

One of my favorite memories of Champ is his love for bubbles—yes, *bubbles!* One day, I got a bubble machine, and when those bubbles started floating around the yard, Champ went crazy chasing them. He leaped and snapped at the bubbles with so much joy. Watching him jump and twist made me laugh until my sides hurt. It was impossible to feel stressed with Champ's silly antics.

Inspired by Champ, I decided to bring more play into my life. I even started going to my granddaughter's bubble bus parties during her birthday weekend each year. These parties were magical—bubbles everywhere, kids laughing and playing, and me joining in, feeling like a kid again. Bubbles have a way of making you forget your worries and just have fun.

These bubble-filled moments became the best part of my days, helping me face challenges with a lighter heart. Adding fun and joyful activities to your daily routine will allow you to live more fully and happily. Follow Champ's example and let your inner "Staffy" guide you to a life full of play and laughter.

Here is a Champ Challenge for you: Go out and buy some bubbles! Have a blast chasing them and letting go of your worries. And remember to visit our social media page and share your photo and adventure with all of us!

Woof Wisdom: Champ's Joyful Living

"Woof woof, friend! It's time to yodel like a Staffy! Get outside, sniff the flowers, and roll around in the grass. If you can't go out, brighten your space with fresh flowers, air, and light. Show those pearly whites and smile often, letting joy fill your heart. Let's wag our tails and have a blast together!"

Wrapping Up Trick #7: Wag Your Tail and Have Fun Doing It

Living with enthusiasm and joy, inspired by a dog like Champ, can change your entire experience. Practice adding fun and joy into your daily life, encourage others to stay happy, and embrace adventure and excitement for each new day.

Living with spirit and fun isn't just a mindset—it's a way of life that can transform everything. Adopting a playful attitude like Champ can fill your days with passion, excitement, and happiness. Throughout this chapter, we've shared tips to help you bring more fun and joy into your routine. Whether creating a bucket list, setting goals for pleasure, or smiling like a Champ, these practices can make every day feel like a new chance for happiness.

Living with joy and enthusiasm means more than just having fun—*embracing every moment with an open heart and a lighthearted spirit.* Champ has shown us that life is too short to take too seriously. His cheerful demeanor can bring us joy for ourselves and those around us.

So, *wag your tail and have fun doing it!* Treat life as an adventure and make every moment count. As you use these lessons, you'll find that happiness isn't just a destination—it's a way of life.

Next, get ready for another exciting journey. The upcoming chapter will explore Trick #8: *Finding Your Paws and Peace Zone.* Just as our furry friends find balance and grace even when life gets *ruff,* we'll learn how to stay balanced through life's puddles. So, let's discover the art of balance in our lives and keep this tail-wagging adventure going strong!

CHAPTER 15

TRICK #8 – FINDING YOUR PAWS AND PEACE ZONE

How do you find balance when things are really *ruff? Meet Willing The Wonder Dog,* one of Champ's pit bull friends. Willing faced many physical challenges: one leg amputated, a peg leg, elbow problems in both front legs, and a fused spine. Despite this, he lived a life of *pawpose* and balance. Rescued from *death row,* he worked as a therapy dog in a reading program at an elementary school in Delaware, bringing joy and inspiration to many children.

Willing's story shows us that no matter how hard life gets, finding balance within ourselves can help us reach our *pawtential.* Even with his physical limits, Willing found inner peace and balance, allowing him to live a full life. This chapter will teach you how to find balance, unlock your *pawtential,* and overcome obstacles. You can handle life's chaos with grace and resilience by creating harmony within, just like Willing.

In this chapter, we will step into the *paws and peace zone*—a special place inside you where everything feels calm and balanced. Here, you find the strength to face challenges with confidence and tranquility. Like Willing, when we discover our *paws and peace zone,* we can overcome obstacles and live joyfully.

Join us as we explore Willing's 'tail' and learn how to achieve balance, no matter what life throws at us!

Paws for Balance: Story Time with Champ and Willing

Observing the incredible resilience of *Willing The Wonder Dog* has deeply influenced my understanding of balance and inner peace. Although I never met Willing, his story and spirit touched my life countless times. Seeing his social media posts and reading updates about this amazing dog, with all his physical challenges, moving with determination and grace, left me in awe. Despite his so-called limitations, Willing radiated a sense of calm and contentment. He didn't focus on what he lacked but embraced what he had, living each day with *pawpose* and joy.

One specific day stands out in my memory. I was feeling overwhelmed and stressed with the demands of my daily life, juggling various responsibilities and feeling the weight of my limitations. That day, I saw a Facebook post showing Willing inspiring a group of children from the elementary school where he served as a therapy dog. I could see the sparkle in his eyes as he interacted with the kids in a reading program.

Seeing Willing in that photo, I was struck by his ability to remain balanced and centered despite his physical challenges. It was as if he had found a way to tap into an inner reservoir of peace and passion that transcended his external circumstances. His presence reminded me of the importance of finding stillness and harmony within myself, regardless of the chaos around me.

Champ has also been a huge inspiration for my journey toward balance and inner peace. His ability to live in the moment and enjoy life has taught me to let go of stress and focus on the present. One day, I was feeling overwhelmed and frustrated. Champ noticed and brought his favorite toy over, nudging me to play. His playful energy made me smile and forget my worries for a while.

Insights on Finding Your Paws and Peace Zone

The *paws and peace zone* is a place of inner calm and balance within ourselves. It's where we feel peaceful and steady, helping us handle life's challenges with ease and strength.

Think of the *paws and peace zone* as a peaceful spot inside you, like the calm center of a storm. Finding this stillness helps you see things clearly, make good decisions, and move through life confidently and peacefully.

The idea of yin and yang energies is a great way to understand this balance. Yin and yang represent opposite forces, like light and darkness, or rest and activity. We feel more stable and stronger when these energies are balanced inside us. Willing balanced his physical challenges with his inner strength, demonstrating how he harmonized his yin and yang energies. This balance allowed him to find stability and live a fulfilling life despite his difficulties, showing us that we can achieve the same balance and resilience.

Sometimes, obstacles seem huge, but many are just in our minds, created by fear and doubt. Finding our inner balance allows us to see past these illusions and realize our *pawtential*. Willing's story shows us that what we see as limitations can help us discover our strengths and grow.

Finding this inner balance is essential for spreading peace and harmony to others. When we feel centered and balanced, it affects all parts of our lives. Our relationships improve because we become more patient and understanding. Our work feels more meaningful because we approach it with clarity and *pawpose*. Our overall happiness improves because we maintain a state of inner peace.

Imagine starting your day with calm and balance, carrying that peace through everything you do. You handle challenges with a clear mind and a steady heart. You respond to stress with grace and patience. This is the power of finding your *paws and peace zone*. It's not about avoiding

127

problems but about handling them with inner strength, *pawsitively* affecting every part of your life.

Champ's Trick in Action #8: "Finding Your Paws and Peace Zone"

Hey, furry friends, it's time to put Champ's wisdom into practice! Here are some *pawsome* suggestions to help you achieve inner balance:

- **Paws and Pose:** Set aside a few minutes daily for yoga or light stretching. Picture yourself finding balance and peace, just like a dog stretching and finding their *pawfect* relaxing spot. Engage in light physical activities like a short walk or a quick workout to help you feel more balanced and energized.

- **Wag In Yin/Yang Balance**: Pay attention to your energies and strive for balance. When you feel too wound up *(excess yang),* engage in calming activities like reading or gentle stretching. If you're feeling sluggish *(excess yin),* get moving with a brisk walk or a playful activity. Find your balance just like a dog shaking off a nap.

- **Sniff Out Mental Illusions**: Identify thoughts and beliefs that create *pawceived* limitations. Question their validity just as a dog sniffs out every corner, replacing negative thoughts with empowering and *pawsitive* truths.

- **Zen-ful Journaling**: Keep a journal to document your daily efforts to find your *Zen zone*. Reflect on your meditation, visualization, and balancing practices. Note any mental illusions you overcome and the *pawsitive* outcomes from these practices.

Adding these *pawsitive* practices to your daily routine shows how amazing finding your *paws and peace zone* can be. Let Champ's wisdom and Willing's inspiration help you find inner balance and harmony to handle life's challenges like a pro. So, take a deep breath and find calm as you start this journey to inner tranquility.

Woof Wisdom: Champ's Balanced Approach

"Woof woof, friend! It's time to dig deep and find your paws and peace zone. Every day, take a moment to do something pawstive to help you find balance. Imagine a peaceful spot where everything feels right, like when I find my favorite sunny spot to nap. Focus on balancing your yin/yang energies – notice when you feel off and take steps to get back on track. And remember, the only limits you have are the ones you believe in. Challenge those pesky thoughts and replace them with pawsitive ones. Let's find that balance and live life to the fullest, just like my buddy Willing did daily!"

Wrapping Up Trick #8: Finding Your Paws and Peace Zone

Now that we've explored *Trick #8*, let's dive into Champ's tail-wagging wisdom and draw inspiration from Willing. *Finding your paws and peace zone* and balancing your energies isn't just a practice—it's a way of being that can transform your entire life.

By adopting these suggestions, you can fill your life with the peace, balance, and resilience needed to face life's challenges.

Willing has shown us that inner balance is not about living a life free of challenges but about finding harmony within ourselves despite those obstacles. Following his example and practicing Champ's strategies can create a life that resonates with inner stillness and satisfaction.

Use the insights and tools from this chapter to find your inner balance. Let these practices guide you to a peaceful and harmonious life, one mindful breath at a time.

In the next chapter, we'll learn how mastering these *8 Tricks* helps you enjoy the rewards of your journey. Like our furry friends, get ready to unlock your full *pawtential* and live without limits. Let's go and discover how to be our best selves and unleash our greatness!

CHAPTER 16

UNLEASHING THE REWARDS: THE POWER OF CHAMP'S 8 TIMELESS TRICKS

Who let the dogs out? Woof, woof! It's time to unleash the ultimate rewards of mastering *Champ's 8 Timeless Tricks!* In this chapter, we're diving into the treasures that await when you fully embrace these timeless lessons, bringing joy, freedom, and fulfillment into your life.

Imagine the exhilaration of a dog released from the confines of a leash—bounding with excitement, feeling the wind in its fur, and relishing every moment of newfound freedom. That's the essence of what these tricks can bring into your life. It's about living with the *unbridled* enthusiasm and joy that dogs naturally exude, making every day an adventure.

Since Champ's passing, my journey has been a blend of sorrow and profound evolution. Losing his physical presence shattered my heart, yet it also paved the way for a deeper comprehension of his teachings. By practicing Champ's *timeless tricks,* I've evolved, embracing life's challenges and joys with a renewed sense of *pawpose.* His spirit continues to lead me, filling me with anticipation for the future and a belief that I can conquer anything.

As we *emBARK* on this chapter, let's revel in the joy of breaking free from our own mental limitations, discovering a life of abundance and royal treatment, and ultimately finding ourselves dog-gone happy, and living on *pawpose.*

Escape Your Own Mental Dog Pound!

When we master *Champ's 8 Timeless Tricks,* we unlock the gate to personal freedom, gaining a fresh *pawspective* on life. This freedom isn't just about physical liberation; it's about freeing our minds from the constraints of fear, doubt, and self-judgment. Just as Champ enthusiastically leaped into each day, we can embrace each moment with a sense of endless *pawsibility.*

Mastering these tricks empowers us to build resilience and self-confidence, giving us the strength to confront the tough questions about our circumstances. *Are we hostages to our situations, or can we break free from the invisible fences of our minds?* Champ's wisdom shows us that true happiness comes from within, and by choosing happiness, we gain the courage to make necessary changes in our lives.

Take a moment to reflect on your own life:

- Are you a pup caught in a kennel of circumstances?
- Are you allowing fear and doubt to leash your mind?
- What changes can you make to break free from these mental constraints and run free like a happy dog?

Champ taught me that happiness is an inside job. Observing him find joy in the simplest things—chasing butterflies, sniffing flowers, or just lying in the sun—reminded me that we can choose happiness. It's about shifting our *pawspective* and seeing the beauty in everyday moments. Inspired by Champ, I learned to break free from my own mental pound, letting go of worries and embracing each day's pleasures.

Just as Champ transformed from a scrawny runt into a wise and strong *Staffie,* we too can undergo a transformation. When we let go of our fears and the limits we put on ourselves, it's like a dog breaking free from its leash and running wild with newfound freedom.

Are you ready to escape your own mental dog pound?

Get Ready for Tons of Pawsome "Treat"ment

Living by *Champ's 8 Timeless Tricks* offers countless rewards. One of the most important lessons I've learned from mastering these tricks is being open and ready to receive. Just like a dog eagerly waiting for a treat, we need to be receptive to the rewards our efforts bring. This openness allows good things to flow into our lives.

To truly enjoy life's treats, it's essential to let go of specific expectations and the fear of what might happen. When we cling to strict expectations, we limit the *pawssibilities*. Instead, trusting that good things will come in unexpected ways opens us up to greater rewards.

By focusing on love and abundance rather than fear and scarcity, we align ourselves with the universe's flow, making it easier to attract incredible blessings. Champ was a great example of this. He didn't worry about how he'd get his treats; he simply knew they would come. I remember how thrilled he was when he received a surprise package from his fur-friend Mia, filled with treats. This moment showed that rewards can arrive in surprising and delightful ways. Champ's approach to life taught me to replace expectations with gratitude.

Pawsitive Power: Wagging into the Law of Attraction

Using the law of attraction is like fetching the ultimate tennis ball—you just need to ask, believe, and be ready to catch it. Here's how it works, doggy style:

- **Ask**: Clearly bark out what you desire. Make sure the universe hears your 'woof' loud and clear.

- **Believe**: Trust that you deserve all the best treats life offers. Know in your doggy heart that it's coming your way.

- **Receive**: Be ready to catch those blessings with open *paws,* like a dog waiting for a treat.

When we set our intentions with clarity and trust, we align with the universe's abundant flow, just like a well-trained pup aligning with its favorite human. Embrace the tail-wagging joy of knowing that the universe has your back (and belly rubs) covered.

Be Dog-gone Happy "On Pawpose"

The ultimate reward of mastering *Champ's 8 Timeless Tricks* is discovering and living your *pawpose.* When you live on *pawpose,* every action and decision is filled with meaning and deep satisfaction.

True enjoyment starts from within. It's not just about what happens around us but how we engage with the world. Champ taught me that one of the best ways to maintain a "Staffy" smile is by helping others. Bringing happiness to others makes us feel happier and spreads *pawsitivity.*

Joy is contagious. When we're joyful and *pawsitive,* we brighten up everyone around us. Our smiles and kindness create a ripple effect. Champ's constant enthusiasm reminded me of the power of a simple smile and a wagging tail. Sometimes, we look outside ourselves for validation, forgetting that our true *pawtential* is within us. By connecting with our highest *pawpose,* we uncover the unique talents and passions we can share with the world.

Champ was an incredible guide on this path. He showed me that happiness isn't a final destination but a way of living. His enthusiasm and our *100-Day Smile Challenge* demonstrated that fulfilling a *pawpose* brings deep joy and happiness and is an ongoing journey we experience daily.

Fulfillment Exercise: "Purposeful Paws"

To help you stay connected to the lessons and maintain your happiness, here's a simple exercise:

- **Reflect:** Spend a few minutes each day reflecting on what brings you joy and fulfillment.

- **Serve:** Identify one small way to serve others or contribute *pawsitively* to someone's day.

- **Celebrate:** Celebrate your progress and the impact you're making, no matter how small.

Woof Wisdom: *"Woof woof, friends! It's time to find your pawpose and spread happiness like a "Staffy" smile. Look within, discover your unique gifts, and use them to make the world a better place. Serve others, make them smile, and you'll find that your own happiness grows. Let's wag our tails and light up the world together!"*

Bone-us Treats:

- Practice serving others and making a *pawsitive* impact daily.
- Engage in activities that help you connect with your inner gifts and highest *pawpose*.
- Put your energy into things that give you a sense of satisfaction.

Unleashing the Wisdom of Man's Best Friend

Champ has gifted us his *8 Timeless Tricks*. These tricks aren't just tips for happiness—they're *keys* to unlocking abundance: happiness, peace, and freedom. By mastering these tricks, we tap into the wisdom of man's best friend, discovering compassion, strength, and the rewards that come from living a life filled with joy and purpose.

Mastering Champ's tricks is a journey of growth and learning. Each trick has taught us something important: living in the moment, letting go of the past, trusting our instincts, and loving ourselves.

Keep practicing these *8 Timeless Tricks*. Let them become a natural part of your life, sustaining your sense of well-being and contentment. Remember, your actions and mindset shape your reality, and you have the power to create the life you want.

Woof Wisdom: *"Woof woof, dear friends! Keep in mind, life's journey is best enjoyed with an open heart and a playful spirit. Let my tricks guide you to a pawpose-filled life. You've got the wisdom of man's best friend within you—unleash it and let your light shine!"*

Bone-us Treats:

- Reflect on the *8 Timeless Tricks* and how they can transform your life.
- Practice each trick daily, allowing the wisdom to become second nature.
- Celebrate your journey and the new *leash* on life you've discovered.

Embracing the Treats of Mastering Champ's 8 Timeless Tricks

As we wag our way to the end of this chapter and trot into part three of *Champ The Human Whisperer,* let's celebrate our incredible journey so far. We've dug deep into *Champ's Timeless Tricks,* discovering profound lessons that can truly transform our lives. These insights empower us to live a dog-gone happy life *on pawpose.*

This isn't the end, but a new beginning. You have the tools, the guidance, and the spirit of a true champion within you. Now, go out there and live your best life, embracing the essence of the *Human Whisperer* in your own furry friend and spreading happiness wherever you go.

As we leap into the next part, *Champ's Golden Years - Reflections and Farewell,* we're shifting gears to peek behind the scenes of Champ's everyday life. We'll honor his legacy, reflect on his golden years, and prepare for the final farewell. This part of the book will guide you in embracing and accepting change, ensuring the wisdom of man's best friend continues to inspire and uplift you.

PART THREE

CHAMP'S GOLDEN YEARS: REFLECTIONS AND FAREWELL

CHAPTER 17

CHAMP'S GOLDEN YEARS: ADAPTING AS A CHAMPION OF CHANGE

Our journey evolved as Champ entered his senior years, bringing new dimensions of love, care, and experience. This time wasn't just about his changing behavior and health but also about adapting to the challenges that came with them. Champ truly embodied the qualities of a champion—resilient and adaptable. These golden years taught me invaluable lessons in patience and the importance of appreciating every moment. Caring for an aging dog is a rollercoaster of emotions— heartwarming, heart-wrenching, and everything in between.

Imagine a once lively and spirited dog moving a bit slower with a spirit that remains just as bright. Each gray hair and more deliberate step is a testament to the passage of time and the enduring strength of our bond. These years brought a new rhythm to our lives, filled with gentler moments and quieter joys, revealing the true essence of companionship and the beauty of embracing change.

Reflecting on Champ's senior years, it's clear how much our routines shifted, our activities adapted, and our love deepened. Caring for him during this period involved practical adjustments and profound emotional engagement, reminding me to cherish every moment and prepare for the inevitable farewell.

For Champ and any aging dog, these golden years remind us that life is ever-evolving. They teach us to embrace change with grace and compassion. Adapting to the needs of our aging pets also helps us learn to adapt to changes in our lives. Through sharing these experiences, I hope to offer insights and inspiration to others walking a similar path with their beloved pets, showing that the golden years can be some of the most meaningful of all.

Reflecting on Champ's Personal Changes and Needs

Champ's once effortless leaps and bounds gradually became more measured and deliberate without a specific moment marking the change. The first notable shift was the development of lower back arthritis, which began to affect his mobility. As a chiropractor and energy healer, I was keenly aware of the pain this condition could cause. To help alleviate his discomfort, Champ received regular chiropractic adjustments and Reiki energy healing sessions, a Japanese technique that promotes relaxation and healing. I would massage his stiff joints and sore muscles almost daily, providing relief and ensuring he felt loved and cared for.

Over time, Champ also became more intuitive about his dietary needs, gradually rejecting processed dry dog food in favor of homemade meals. To support his overall health, I transitioned him to a raw vegetable-based diet, supplemented with boiled chicken, rice, goat's milk, mussels, and eggs—foods he loved. Initially, Champ was on a frozen raw food diet, but it frequently caused him to spit or throw up as it got stuck in his throat. Determined to find a solution, I meticulously monitored his tolerance and regularly adjusted his meal plan. I even began praying over his food, blessing it with energy and vitality. Champ would bow his head during the prayer, patiently waiting before eating, and he became accustomed to waiting for the last bite from my plate.

Despite our efforts, Champ developed chronic ear infections, which eventually led to complete deafness. However, I never stopped talking to him as if he could still hear me, maintaining our unspoken bond through gestures and touch.

Lessons from Champ's Ability to Adapt and Change

Reflecting on these changes, I see how profoundly they shaped our lives. Every adjustment—whether in Champ's diet, mobility, or daily routines—was a testament to the love and dedication that defined our bond. These years taught me that patience isn't just a virtue; it's essential. Adaptability became our new normal, and the beauty of unconditional love shone through every challenge we faced.

The evolving needs of aging dogs offer valuable lessons for our own lives. As we adapt to our dog's changing needs, we can learn to embrace the changes in our lives. These lessons guide us to navigate life's transitions with grace and resilience. Dogs, with their ability to wag through it all, remind us that even in life's shadows, there's always something to smile about—especially if there's a treat involved!

Balancing Activity with Health Constraints

Finding the right balance between giving Champ the necessary exercise and not overstraining him was a constant challenge. Our walks became more leisurely, focusing on his comfort and enjoyment rather than covering long distances.

Hiking routines had to be adapted to accommodate Champ's health constraints. I chose trails that were easier for him to navigate and avoided steep or rocky paths that could strain his joints. During our walks, I paid close attention to his energy levels and took frequent breaks to let him rest. Champ's spirit remained unbroken, and he continued to enjoy our outdoor adventures.

Emotionally, it was difficult for me to accept the changes in our shared activities. Champ had always been my loyal hiking and running partner, and it was challenging to come to terms with the fact that those days were behind us. Yet, in these moments, I found joy in the simple pleasures: watching him sniff every interesting scent, seeing his tail wag with curiosity, and rejoicing that he still had a smile. His age didn't stop people from doing double-takes and craning their necks to watch him strut his stuff. Most people couldn't believe he was 14. Champ always retained his ability to make people smile even at his slower pace.

Champ had his own unique way of making our walks memorable. He would mope, go out, move slowly, and take his time—but he was ready to run when we turned around to go home. Sometimes, I had to remind him that he couldn't do everything he used to. His inner spirit would come out like a wild wolf, wanting to race up the stairs when we got home, even though he sometimes couldn't walk without a limp.

Insights from Balancing Activities with Health Constraints

Just as I had to find the right balance for Champ's activities, we, too, must find balance in our own lives, especially when faced with physical or emotional limitations. By embracing these changes and focusing on the joy in simple moments, we can navigate life's transitions with dignity and strength. Champ's journey reminds us that even as circumstances change, our spirit can remain strong, and we can continue to bring joy to ourselves and others.

Champ's Constant Presence and Involvement in Daily Life

Champ desired to be involved in everything I did throughout his life. Whether I was working at my desk, cooking in the kitchen, or simply lying on the couch, Champ would always find a way to insert himself into the activity. And when I practiced yoga, he never missed an opportunity to show off his downward dog. His antics always brought a smile to my face.

His inquisitive nature and eagerness to participate in daily routines were constant reminders that teamwork makes the dream work. Champ had a knack for making even mundane tasks feel like shared adventures. His presence was a blend of endearing interference and genuine help, as if he believed his presence was indispensable (and of course it was)!

Champ took his job as my 24/7 fur bodyguard very seriously. If I moved, he moved; if I stayed still, he remained still. His pack dynamic was essential to his well-being, and I made every effort to ensure that he was rarely left alone.

I cherished every moment with Champ. When he lay on my towel while I was in the bathtub, I would get another one so he wouldn't have to move. When he was younger, he would run in when he heard me open the coconut oil jar to apply it like lotion after a shower. I had to strategically use it and get dressed, or he would lick my legs faster than I could apply it. Sometimes, he would fall asleep in front of the sink while I was in the tub. I would carefully walk around or straddle over him. Some days, I would touch him while he lay there as I put on makeup, feeling the flow of our energy syncing together.

His stunts were off the charts. As previously mentioned, *Staffies* are known for their *huff,* wearing their emotions on their paws. Champ would dig his bed at night and then plop down. If he didn't like something, he would turn up his nose, and if he was emotional, you would get the *Staffy huff.*

Champ had gone to puppy training and knew his commands well. He walked on my right side and heeled perfectly. But in his later years, I allowed him to be himself and honored his needs on our walks. When walking with someone else, Champ often needed clarification about whom to follow, glancing between us for direction. He would usually walk slightly ahead, turning his head from side to side like Rudolph the Red-Nosed Reindeer, making sure we were both there and everything was okay.

The Value of Companionship: Lessons from Champ's Daily Involvement

Champ's constant presence and involvement in daily activities teach us the value of being fully engaged in the moment. Like Champ, we can learn to immerse ourselves in our daily routines, finding joy and connection in the simplest tasks. His adaptability, even as his needs changed, reminds us to remain flexible and open to new ways of doing things.

Champ shows us the importance of staying connected with those we love, being present, and making the most out of every moment. His ability to adapt and find joy in every situation inspires us to approach our lives similarly.

Reflecting on Changes in Sleeping Patterns

During Champ's final couple of months, he started to sleep more and preferred spending time alone, in drastic contrast to his younger years when he was always by my side.

His increased need for rest coincided with a period of deep healing in my own life. After a lifelong battle with sleep disorders, I spent two years intentionally healing to get my body to rest deeply. Interestingly, Champ's sleep patterns mirrored my own. As I worked on getting better rest, Champ also began to sleep more deeply and appeared more relaxed during his naps.

While I missed having Champ as my constant shadow, I understood that his body needed extra rest to cope with the physical toll of aging. Mornings often felt like trying to wake a sleepy schoolchild. Champ would stubbornly stay in bed, preferring the comfort of his blankets over starting the day. His reluctance to get up was a humorous reminder of his unique personality and the need for patience and understanding during this stage of his life.

I cherished the less-frequent moments when Champ sought me. Occasionally, he'd wake from a deep sleep, realize I was not there, and start searching for me. He'd check the bathroom first, then the bedroom, and finally my office. If he didn't find me, he would determinedly start the search again. His persistent and somewhat comical routine always brought a smile to my face.

I would take intentional "bubby breaks" during busy days to get centered, grounded, and connect deeply with him. These breaks allowed me to enjoy my days without rushing, balancing productivity with peace and *pawpose.*

144

Lessons from Champ's Changing Sleep Patterns

As we observe our pets' natural progression of aging, we can learn to adapt to the changing needs and rhythms in our own lives. Just as Champ needed more rest and a slower pace, we, too, can recognize when it's time to pause, rest, and recharge.

By accepting and accommodating these changes, we practice patience and compassion with our pets and ourselves. Champ's ability to adapt to his need for more sleep teaches us the importance of listening to our bodies and respecting our needs. Despite his increased need for rest, his persistent search for me reminds us of the importance of maintaining connections and nurturing relationships, even as circumstances change.

Adapting to Life in Sedona: A New Chapter

In Champ's last few months, we made a significant move to Sedona, AZ. I had concerns about traveling with an elderly dog, especially one who had always been so attached to his familiar surroundings. I worried about how he would respond to the new environment and whether the change would overwhelm him.

To my surprise and relief, Champ quickly adapted to our new home. Sedona's vibrant landscape and serene atmosphere rejuvenated him. Despite his age, Champ embraced the new surroundings with curiosity and enthusiasm. Watching him figure out new spots to do his business, considering there was virtually no grass in Sedona, was quite comical.

One of the most encouraging signs was Champ's gradual improvement in his ability to walk up and down hills. The terrain in Sedona differed from what he was used to, but he managed to navigate it with determination. Though our walks were shorter, Champ enjoyed exploring the new territory, and the change of scenery brought him a renewed sense of vitality. The magic of Sedona's landscape seemed to heal him, enhancing his quality of life.

Reflecting on Champ's experience, we learn that change, though often difficult, can bring new opportunities for joy and fulfillment. His journey encourages us to embrace life's transitions with an open heart and a *pawsitive* outlook, knowing that each change carries the *pawtential* for new adventures and personal transformation.

A Guardian's Love: Champ's Protective Instincts

Champ was always protective of me. When he was younger, he didn't like anyone hugging me or showing affection—he wanted all the attention for himself. Over time, I realized his intuition guided him; he seemed to know when someone wasn't right for me. I used to believe that Champ would be the one to pick my soul partner, and when he finally accepted someone loving me, I'd know that person was right for me.

When I entered a new relationship, Champ was initially apprehensive, but with time, he accepted my partner. Champ even began to care for my partner like he cared for me. It was as though Champ understood this person was there to help, especially in his final days. My partner played a significant role, assisting me both physically and emotionally as Champ's health declined. He would often take Champ on his morning walks and make his breakfast daily, even though he was vegan, and handling raw food wasn't a problem. His willingness to share in Champ's care meant the world to me.

I later realized that this support system not only eased the burden during Champ's final days but also helped me transition after his passing. By sharing the responsibilities, my daily routine subtly changed, making it easier to cope with losing my dear companion.

Lessons from Champ's Protective Instincts

Champ's protective instincts teach us about the deep, intuitive connections dogs form with their human companions. His behavior wasn't just about seeking attention; it was his way of safeguarding his loved ones. Over time, it became clear that dogs have a keen sense of who is suitable for us, acting like guardian angels in fur. When Champ finally accepted my partner, it was a significant moment that taught me to trust his judgment and understand that pets often *pawceive* our needs better than we do. Champ's acceptance allowed me to welcome new relationships into my life without feeling it would diminish our bond. His actions highlight the balance between guarding our hearts and allowing them to grow, showing that true love isn't *pawssessive* but inclusive. We can be always looking out for our best interests while being open to new *pawssibilities.*

Celebrating Champ's 14th Birthday

On January 28, 2024, Champ turned 14, and we celebrated this milestone with a special party. The theme was *Get Wild,* featuring animal figures on the wall and a palm tree centerpiece with a playful monkey. It was a joyous occasion filled with love and laughter, and Champ's excitement was contagious.

We treated Champ to his favorite foods, including a bowl of whipped cream, which he devoured with delight. He had always loved attending children's parties and would often become the life of the event. This party was no different, despite his age.

The party was not just about the festivities but a heartfelt celebration of Champ's remarkable life and the joy he had brought to so many. He eagerly opened his presents. I always loved how excited he got to receive gifts. It had been a while since we last threw a party for him, and deep inside, I knew that celebrating his 14th Birthday was a way to honor his legacy and the countless memories we had created together.

I am grateful for the time we shared celebrating him. Champ's party was a beautiful reminder of the love and happiness he brought into my life and the lives of others. It was a fitting tribute to a loyal companion who had given so much and continued to inspire even in his elder years.

Lessons from Champ's Birthday Celebration

Champ's celebration teaches us to appreciate the present, celebrate milestones, and create lasting memories with our pets. It also inspires us to *get wild* and embrace the excitement and happiness of life's special occasions. By celebrating enthusiastically, we honor the love and joy our pets bring into our lives and acknowledge their unique and irreplaceable roles.

Deepening Our Bond: Highlights from Champ's Golden Years

As Champ's golden years unfolded, our relationship deepened in ways I hadn't anticipated. The lively pup with endless fuel became a gentle soul who treasured quiet moments by my side. This period brought a new depth to our connection, marked by intimate, shared experiences and a mutual understanding that words could never capture.

In these serene moments, I reflected on the immense joy and comfort Champ had brought into my life. New rituals that honored our connection reinforced our bond. One of our favorite rituals was lying in his dog bed together, where Champ would gaze deeply into my eyes as if to say, *"Momma, I don't want to leave you, but it's time for me to enter the next phase of my journey. This one, I must go alone."*

As we transitioned to this heart-wrenching realization, I began to understand the profound lessons Champ was imparting about acceptance, love, and letting go.

Finding Peace and Preparing for the Final Farewell

Accepting the reality of Champ's eventual passing was an emotional journey that required immense strength and grace. The thought of life without him was almost unbearable, but I knew I had to prepare myself both emotionally and physically for the inevitable. My top priority was ensuring Champ's final years were filled with care and comfort. I adjusted our routines to accommodate his needs, made his favorite meals, and provided extra cuddles and attention. Every decision I made was guided by the desire to give him the best *pawssible* quality of life.

The thought of contemplating assisted euthanasia weighed heavily on my heart. I always said that if it came time to make such a decision, I wouldn't be able to do it. The mere thought of it filled me with dread and sorrow. Yet, I knew that part of loving Champ meant being willing to let go when the time was right.

One of the most complex parts of this journey was finding peace. I worked on accepting that death is a natural part of life and that releasing Champ from any potential suffering was an act of love. I wanted his final moments to be peaceful, surrounded by the comfort and security of our bond. During his last few months, I focused on creating a serene environment for him, filling our home with soft music when leaving him home alone. I even prayed with him to let him know that the angels would take good care of him while I was gone.

As the days passed, Champ's presence became an even brighter guiding light in my life. I felt his spirit communicating with me, reassuring me that everything would be okay. I sensed his understanding and acceptance. His eyes, filled with wisdom and love, conveyed a sense of peace that helped me find my own.

Preparing for Champ's transition was one of the most challenging experiences of my life, but it was also profoundly transformative. It taught me the power of humility and the beauty of letting go with grace. Our bond transcended the physical realm, and I knew that, even after his passing, Champ's spirit would continue to guide and inspire me. But that didn't make my human self feel any better.

Looking back over the years, I realize that nothing could prepare me for the eventual farewell to my best friend, because forever would not have been long enough. Recently, someone shared a comforting thought with me: *dogs can't stay forever because they give all they have, and eventually, they have nothing left to give.* This *pawspective* gave me peace.

Reflecting on this journey, I am grateful for our shared time and the profound lessons Champ taught me. His golden years were a testament to the enduring power of unconditional love. Our sacred bond remained unbroken, transcending the boundaries of life and death.

Gather your strength as we honor Champ's life and celebrate his hero's journey. Together, we will navigate the heart-wrenching yet meaningful steps toward his final farewell. Grab a box of tissues, and let's embrace this heartfelt journey.

CHAPTER 18

A HERO'S FAREWELL: CHAMP'S FINAL JOURNEY

Every great love story eventually concludes, yet some endings leave a lasting mark on our hearts. The final chapter of Champ's journey is a testament to his profound paw print on my life and the world. Losing Champ felt like losing a piece of my soul.

For years, I anticipated that saying goodbye to my best friend would be the hardest challenge of my life—and I have faced many. This chapter is not merely a recounting of those last moments; it is a tribute to a loyal friend, a story of deep gratitude for every lesson Champ taught, every wag of his tail, and every moment of joy he brought into my life. As you read these final words, I hope you sense the depth of our connection and the enduring legacy of love that Champ has left behind.

Champ was more than a companion; he was a hero, a true champion who faced life's challenges with unwavering courage and a grateful heart. His life was a beacon of hope, bringing light to even the darkest moments. Champ's journey embodied resilience, love, and joy from a high-spirited pup to a wise elder. His presence touched countless lives and spread a message of happiness and unity.

Join me as I recount our final memories together, the heart-wrenching moments of his passing, and the incredible journey of tenderness and healing that followed. This is Champ's final gift to us all—a reminder that love endures beyond physical presence and that the bonds we share with our beloved companions are everlasting.

The Biggest Lesson of My Life: Vulnerability

Leading up to his crossing the rainbow bridge, there were days when I would crawl into Champ's oversized dog bed and lay there, giving gratitude for every breath he took. Every day was another gift. On days when he didn't feel well, I would lay beside him and cry. I was the little girl who never wanted to be seen crying. If I got emotional listening to a song that touched me, I would hold back my tears and cover my head so no one could see me.

I had always envisioned myself having a complete breakdown and just letting out all my emotions, but I didn't know how to open up that much and be that vulnerable. As the years passed, I got closer to understanding how healing it would be to do just that. Somehow, I knew that Champ would be the one to make it happen.

And he did. His presence and love provided a safe space to explore my vulnerability. Through him, I learned the beauty of expressing my true feelings, the strength in being open and truly seen, and the healing that comes from letting go.

In his final days, Champ showed me it's okay to cry, to feel deeply, and to share those feelings. This lesson has enriched my relationships and my approach to life.

Let's honor Champ's legacy by embracing vulnerability as we move forward. Champ's example teaches us to connect with our emotions and encourage a more compassionate world.

A Hero's Final Journey

On the day before Champ's transition, I followed my usual routine. Champ, who used to wait by the door when leaving, now had a bed in every room and was peacefully sleeping in my office. I went in to tell him goodbye, and just as I was leaving, I felt the urge to turn on the fan for him in case he got hot. In my hurry, I didn't pray with him as usual.

We were on our way to lead a land journey with clients in Sedona, taking people into the vortexes for healing and transformational work. This particular journey was planned for sunset and was incredibly magical. We ran over time, and suddenly, a strong feeling hit me: we needed to get home to Champ. As the clients asked a few more questions, I grew increasingly anxious. Usually, I wouldn't mind staying longer, but I couldn't get home fast enough. Later, my partner told me he heard a dog yell in his mind and knew it was Champ.

When we arrived home, I rushed inside. Typically, we would find Champ sleeping, and because he couldn't hear, he would jump up and greet us when he realized we were home. I always said, *"We caught you sleeping on the job."*

This time, it was different. We walked in, and Champ was sprawled out in the kitchen, his legs splayed out to the side, shaking. The rug was kicked up and pushed back. I immediately knew something was wrong. When I first got down beside him, I thought his water bowl had spilled all over him because he was wet, his mouth and front legs drenched. But that wasn't the case. He had been drooling, and foam was coming out of his mouth. He was disoriented, and I knew we needed to get him outside. He tried to get up but couldn't, so I started helping him. He tried to take off on his own, but he had no control or strength. We finally got him stable enough to get him outside, and my partner carried him up and down the stairs.

There was a time I never would have moved into a place with stairs because of Champ's back, but I knew I couldn't let that fear stop us from moving into the space that was calling us.

When we came back inside, Champ started going crazy. He tried to get into every corner and bury himself in the walls. He went to places like the space between the headboard and the wall or the kitchen, trying to push his way between the refrigerator and the wall. I put his leash back on him and tried calming him with energy healing. I wanted to give him some CBD oil for dogs to relax him, but he was too restless.

We took him into the bathroom and got him to lie down on one of his beds, and my partner suggested he might be dehydrated. He made some water with Himalayan salt and maple syrup. He spoon-fed it to Champ, and after a while, Champ seemed to regain some sense. We lay with him for a bit and then moved him to the living room to his big bed so I could lie with him. His breath was labored.

It was getting late, so we decided to move him to the bedroom and turn down the lights, hoping he might rest. We pulled him in his bed into the room, but his breathing remained heavy. I could see he was uncomfortable and struggled to move. He tried to reposition himself, and I did my best to ensure he was comfortable.

Needless to say, seeing him like this ripped my soul apart. I felt terrible that he had to go through what he endured all alone, especially because I didn't pray with him before we left. Then, something completely unexpected happened—he started having a seizure. We held him in a way that helped, and my partner tried assisting him to ensure he could breathe. Then he would come to, completely dazed, only to start having another seizure. The seizures picked up in intensity and frequency, until it seemed they were nonstop.

Before the second seizure happened, I tried lying down to see if he would rest. I did not want to have to decide to let him go. But as I watched him, completely out of his mind, his body contracting with one seizure after another, I realized there was no way I could let him suffer like this. Watching him shattered me.

We both stayed up all night with him. I climbed into his bed because I could tell he was looking back to see where I was, while my partner stayed in front of him. I was devastated and falling apart, my soul crying out. I knew I had to get together enough to calm him. At one point, I tried meditating, hoping that if I felt calm, it would calm him down. Then I felt what seemed like a seizure taking over my body, and as I started convulsing, he had his worst seizure yet.

It was a long and gruesome night. By this point, he was drooling blood, and something inside me knew I had to hold myself together for him. Between seizures, I would get up by his face, look him in the eyes, and tell him, *"I am right by you, and I am not going anywhere."* I could feel his soul hanging on as if he didn't want to leave this earth. He was fighting it, so I told him it was safe and I would be okay. I told him it was okay to leave. His seizures had gotten so bad that I thought he was going to transition, and in the back of my mind, I hoped he would make his own choice so I didn't have to.

Champ's struggle through the night was nothing short of heroic. He fought fearlessly; his spirit was determined even amid immense suffering. In those moments, he embodied the essence of a hero on a final journey, displaying courage and tenacity that inspired me to be strong for him.

As I whispered my reassurances, I realized that this was his last, most significant act of love—holding on not for himself but for me, not wanting to leave his loyal companion. Then I heard him whisper, *"Stay strong, Momma, stay strong. I got this! I don't want to leave you, but it is time for you to continue your journey without me. I will be right by your side. I will always be there for you and always be your best friend."*

Champ's final hours were a true testament to the heart of a champion. He faced the final challenge with the same bravery and grace that defined his life. His love, loyalty, and unbreakable spirit will forever be etched in my heart and the hearts of all who were touched by his incredible life.

Seeking Guidance

I began praying and asking for a sign about whether to let Champ go. Then, I realized it was my long-time spiritual mentor, Dr. Wayne Dyer's birthday. I have a deep connection with Wayne, and this felt like a significant sign. Wayne carries the energy of St. Francis, the patron saint of animals. When Champ was returned to me after the trial when he was taken, he had a St. Francis charm on his collar.

I started looking up vets, but Sedona had no overnight options. Being new to the area, Champ wasn't due for his routine visit until the next month. We had previously visited the vet to understand their emergency policy and gather information for an appointment.

At this point, I knew I had to let him go. One of my clients had a vet come to his house for his cat's transition, and I wanted the same for Champ. As daylight broke, I messaged a neighbor, asking her to send healing energy and see if she could find a vet who does house calls through a community group. Champ was in more despair, crying out and yelping from the pain.

We had two vets nearby, one opening at 8 and the other at 9. My gut told me to go across the street, as I felt drawn to her. I believed that was where we were meant to go. So, at 9 am, I called Dr. Martin's office and asked if she could come to our house for euthanasia. They said she does, but only for existing patients, and their earliest appointment was at 2:30 pm. I explained the severity of the situation and asked them to let me know if an earlier slot opened up.

Meanwhile, I called the other vet to see if they could get us in sooner. They didn't do house calls for euthanasia but could see us in 15 minutes. However, with such a short window and considering Champ's fragile condition, we couldn't make it there in time without risking a seizure during the transport. So, I opted to stick with Dr. Martin.

Just as I got off the phone, Dr. Martin's office called back. They had informed her of Champ's condition, and she said they could see us at 10:45 am. We took the appointment. I was so distraught, counting down the moments, knowing my time with Champ was coming to a close. I felt myself going into shock and even trauma watching his little body endure severe seizures repeatedly.

The Final Farewell

We transferred Champ into a smaller bed to make it easier to transport and covered him with his favorite blanket. As we were moving him, he started having another seizure. We arrived a little early and notified the office. They let us in through the back door, taking us straight into a room where they laid down a blanket and propped his head up with a pillow. As soon as we got him there, he started seizing again and began gagging, bringing up blood. Dr. Martin immediately gave him a sedative to stop the seizures, explaining that it would likely only last about 15 minutes before he had another one.

She told us that anytime a dog has a seizure over the age of five, there's a 98% chance they have a brain tumor. These tumors are slow-growing but eventually burst blood vessels, causing brain bleeds that trigger seizures. She explained that if she treated Champ for seizures, he would have less than two months left. She shared that her own dog had experienced the same condition and, despite treatment, had to be euthanized after just two months. I was in disbelief.

My father had had two brain tumors. He lived with them for 30 years, even after two surgeries and overcoming stage 3A lung cancer, but he was finally taken by a seizure he couldn't come out of. He was never the same. One of my uncles had died from a malignant brain tumor. Suddenly, all of Champ's recent behaviors made sense. My dad had wanted to sleep a lot, and my uncle would walk sideways, collapse, and do things out of his mind, like running into walls. I was shocked on so many levels.

I asked the vet if she could come to the house. She said she could, but her schedule didn't allow it that day. She mentioned that the kindest thing I could offer Champ was to let him go that day. They told me we could have everything needed at the clinic, but I wanted it to be peaceful and create a ceremony with music, making it more comfortable for me as well. I had no idea how to respond. I explained to the vet that everything had happened so quickly that I was unsure about the cost and whether I needed to transfer funds to cover it that day. She reassured me that she wasn't concerned about payment then and emphasized that it would be inhumane not to let Champ go. We agreed that I would handle the payment details later. I realized waiting was more for me, and I didn't want Champ to suffer any longer.

Our Unbreakable Bond: Champ's Last Moments

We planned to have Champ cremated. Our neighbor performed a drumming ceremony, sending energy and love his way. I sat with him lying between my legs, spending the next 40 minutes speaking to him, sharing all the great memories, including my being Champ's voice and how he inspired me to write this book. The song *"This Little Light of Mine"* repeatedly played in my head. I said, *"Yes, Bubby, I will finish your book and keep your mission alive. You will make me a superstar, and in doing so, I will keep you alive."* I shared this with the tech who stayed with us, watching in case Champ had another seizure.

I told Champ how he was the best *Bubby* in the whole wide world, how proud I was of all the great work he had done, and thanked him for all the lessons. I also told him that he would be free. Our unbreakable bond was evident in those final moments as we held on to each other with love and gratitude. I found myself expressing my emotions openly in front of complete strangers, something I usually had a hard time doing. I was able to be vulnerable and let my feelings flow freely, honoring the deep connection Champ and I shared. The biggest lesson of my life was accomplished here—I was no longer that little girl hiding under the blanket to cry. Champ had helped me break free.

Finally, the tech asked me if I was ready. I said, *"I will never ever be ready,"* but we knew it was time. Champ was starting to stir, and a seizure was coming on. They gave him another sedative, followed by a stronger one, and then the final shot to euthanize him. I felt like I couldn't take it. Everything was in slow motion, and it was as though the world had stopped. My world felt like it had shattered, and my heart so intensely felt as though it was going to burst.

I watched him as the shots went in. The minute he was gone, without being told, I felt my soul leave my body. I was literally out of my mind. I could visually see every ounce of pain I had stored for lifetimes come bursting out of me as I cried my heart and soul out. I didn't care who heard or saw me. I recall the tech and vet crying, and my partner was behind me, holding me up, but when Champ left, it felt as if I went with him.

I cried and cried, releasing my soul in a way I always knew I needed to. Leaving that day, I was numb, in shock, and in so much pain. It felt as though my body had been through the seizures alongside Champ, my jaws aching from clenching my teeth. All I could hear was his panting, his struggle to breathe, and I kept seeing his body in spasms. The trauma was imprinted in my mind, replaying over and over again. It felt like I was trapped in a nightmare, desperate to wake up.

As I tried to find my footing, I was reminded of the healing work Champ and I had done with others, guiding them through their pain and transformation. This time, I had to turn that wisdom inward, letting Champ's spirit guide me through this profound grief.

Grieving and Healing

In the days that followed, I woke up in tears. Not only did I miss Champ's physical presence, but I couldn't feel his soul. I wondered why; this wasn't how I thought it would be. With my last dog, who was almost 15, I woke up to find her in labored breath at 8:30 am, and by noon, she had transitioned. Everything was organic and quick. Despite the suddenness, I felt her presence immediately after she crossed. This time, however, the experience felt more traumatic, sudden, and devastating.

My physical bond with Champ was stronger, and I expected to still feel him instantly. Instead, I felt more of my own pain, which seemed to block me from connecting with Champ. This added to my grief and confusion, making the loss even more challenging to bear.

Then, I realized that the way to stay connected to Champ was to keep my vibe high and to continue his mission. We had worked on this book for ten years, and I had wanted it done to celebrate with him. But I realized it wouldn't be finished until he crossed the rainbow bridge. So, I poured my pain into his purpose, knowing that was how I would heal. The day after his crossing, I started working on this book again.

As I type this, it has only been four days since his passing. I understand now that the greatest gift of unconditional kindness to him was to take on this pain so he could be free of it. That's what you do for a best friend.

My parents used to tell me that they wished they could carry my burdens for me, but I never really understood what that meant until now. Taking on someone else's pain is the greatest act of unconditional love. We always want our pets to live forever, and in a way, they do—by keeping their love alive inside of us.

Embracing the Pain and Finding Healing

As I navigated the overwhelming grief of losing Champ, I sought to understand the depth of my sorrow. I had experienced death before; losing my dad and sudden losses in my family. Yet, losing Champ felt harder. This profound sense of loss led me to explore the nature of pet grief more deeply. Understanding why losing a pet can be so challenging helped me validate my feelings and find a path toward healing.

Understanding Pet Grief

The following are some reasons why pet loss can be tough:

- **Unconditional Love:** Pets love us unconditionally, without judgment or criticism.

- **Routine and Presence:** Pets are part of our daily routines, making their absence keenly felt.

- **Emotional Support:** Pets provide comfort and emotional support, especially during difficult times.

- **Non-verbal Communication:** The silent understanding and bond shared with pets can be more profound than with humans.

- **Dependence and Care:** The responsibility of caring for a pet creates a deep bond that intensifies the grief when they're gone.

Through my research, I learned that pet grief is real and that it's not uncommon for people to feel this way. In fact, it's normal. Understanding these aspects can help us navigate the complex emotions accompanying pet loss and validate the depth of our grief.

With this understanding, I found solace in knowing that the depth of my sorrow was a testament to the profound bond Champ and I shared—a bond that will never be broken. This knowledge guided me as I continued to navigate my grief and embraced Champ's legacy.

Champ's legacy is of profound love and timeless wisdom. His teachings encapsulated more than just the *8 Timeless Tricks*.

Champ's life and examples to live by have transformed my journey, and I aim to inspire and uplift others. Through sharing our story, I hope to keep his legacy alive.

And just as I told my spiritual mentor Wayne Dyer in 2003, *"As long as I am living, your work will never die,"* I echo the same promise to Champ. *"Bubby, your work and your message will live on through me."*

Farewell, my dearest friend and hero. Until we meet again, I will carry your light within me, spreading your message of unity, happiness, and love to all who will listen. May your mission live on through every smile, every act of kindness, and every moment of connection.

CONCLUSION

A JOURNEY OF LOVE, LESSONS, AND LEGACY

Imagine the climax of an epic movie, where the hero overcomes insurmountable obstacles and defeats the enemy—fears, doubts, and limiting beliefs. The hero's legacy inspires and transforms lives, even after the story ends. As we close this book, let's reflect on the profound impact of *Champ The Human Whisperer* on our hearts and lives. Much like the grand finale of a hero's journey, Champ's story leaves us yearning to carry forward his mission of love, happiness, and transformation.

At the heart of this book is a powerful message: to live with the joy, freedom, and authenticity that Champ embodied daily. He faced adversity fearlessly, displaying an unstoppable spirit and spreading love with every wag of his tail. His commitment, energy, and ability to find happiness in the simplest moments form a blueprint for a fulfilling life. Champ's journey is more than a story of a dog and his owner—it's a guide to living a life full of heart and meaning.

Through *Unleashing the Wisdom of Man's Best Friend*, we've learned profound life lessons about embracing freedom and living in the moment. Champ exemplified how our dogs can be our greatest teachers, showing us true heroism lies in everyday acts of kindness, courage, and steadfast devotion.

Throughout these pages, we've discovered how to awaken our inner Champ, tap into our potential, and learn the ABCs of living like a champion. By practicing the wisdom of dogs, we can become empowered humans, enriching the lives of all dogs and contributing to a more compassionate world.

We've also uncovered *Champ's 8 Timeless Tricks* for living your best life. From "Burying Your Bones by Letting Go" of past burdens to "Living in Pooch Time Consciousness" by embracing the present moment, Champ's wisdom has guided us on a transformative journey. His fearless nature and quick-witted approach to life have taught us invaluable lessons.

From a vulnerable pup to a true champion, Champ's journey is a testament to inner strength, courage, and the power of embracing one's true self. As a bully breed ambassador, he shattered stereotypes, proving that love and kindness can triumph over prejudice. He faced physical challenges and societal biases head-on, emerging triumphant and inspiring us to do the same.

Our exploration of the ancient connection between humans and dogs has shown us that our furry friends have much to teach us about realizing our full potential. This spiritual connection and telepathic bond allow us to communicate with our dogs on a deeper level, understanding their needs and feelings through the love and energy in our hearts. Even after they leave this physical world, their spirit lives on, imprinted on our souls. By embracing and practicing Champ's teachings, we honor his legacy and contribute to a more compassionate world.

A Hero's Sign: Love Never Dies

As I completed this book, striving to keep Champ's smile and spirit alive, I planned a 10th-anniversary repost of the *100-Day Smile Challenge* in his honor. I asked him for a sign to know that he is still by my side through this journey of keeping his legacy alive. *"Show me you are with me, Bubby," I whispered.* Just a few hours later, my friend Kelly, whom Champ knew as Aunt Kelly, sent me a message:

"I just remembered something... not sure if I ever told you this, but remember the 'LOVE.' T-shirt I gave you? When it arrived, there was a hole in one of the letters as if the letter, not the T-shirt, was punctured. I thought, what??? I can't give this to her. Rather than spending time on it, I walked away to do something else, knowing a solution would present itself. A couple of hours later, I picked up the shirt again, and the hole was healed! It had somehow healed itself!!! A random memory, but hoping it is the right time for you to read this!"

I immediately responded:

"OHHHH My Gosh! You didn't tell me this, but the timing is impeccable. I had just asked Champ for a sign and wrote the book's conclusion about how love never ends—it just changes forms! Completing this book is helping mend the hole in my heart and soul."

Kelly had given me this shirt as a tribute to my connection with Dr. Wayne Dyer. He had a series of shirts, one of which was "LOVE." with a period after it. She then reminded me that the period had significance: it meant love is pure, but we complicate love with conditions, and the period indicates pure love. This miraculous message reminded me of the magic and love that continue to surround us, even when we can't see it. Champ's pure, unconditional love exemplifies this perfectly. His love was simple, genuine, and free of complications.

As you put these principles into practice, let Champ's light shine through you. Be the beacon of hope and joy in your own life and in the lives of others. Let your actions be a testament to the love and wisdom Champ imparted, and continue to spread happiness wherever you go.

Continuing Champ's Mission

Champ's mission to spread happiness and unity doesn't end with this book; it continues with you. By embracing and practicing his teachings, you become part of a global movement dedicated to creating a world filled with love and compassion. Join *Global Paws For Peace,* participate in events, and share Champ's message of kindness. Together, we can honor his legacy and make a lasting difference.

As you close this book, carry the essence of Champ's spirit with you. *Practice Champ's 8 Timeless Tricks daily.* Allow yourself to be present, to love deeply, and to find joy in every moment. Embrace challenges with courage and resilience, knowing you can overcome any obstacle.

Here's what you can do to honor his legacy:

- **Spread Happiness**: Emulate Champ's *100-Day Smile Challenge* in your own way. Spread kindness, share smiles, and make the world a brighter place.

- **Advocate for Change:** Promote unity, education, and empathy to influence policy changes and foster fair dog treatment for all dogs.

- **Cherish Every Moment**: Appreciate the simple joys in life and value the time with your loved ones, both human and furry.

- **Live with Purpose**: Find your mission and pursue it intentionally and passionately. Make a positive impact on the world around you.

For more inspiration and to continue Champ's mission, visit GlobalPawsForPeace.org. You can also follow *Champ's Legacy* on his Facebook page and participate in our ongoing initiatives to promote unity, happiness, and love.

By embracing these principles, you too can become a light in the darkness, navigating life's challenges with confidence and courage, and inspiring others to do the same. Champ's legacy embodies unwavering devotion, inner strength, and the incredible connection between humans and their canine companions.

Love's Everlasting Light

In the introduction, I mentioned how Champ's wisdom would guide you through this journey. Now, as you reach the end, remember that you are the one who will continue to inspire others with Champ's spirit. The love, lessons, and insights you've gathered are not just memories—they are tools to help you become a beacon of positivity and strength for others. Champ's example motivates us all to live with purpose, stand up for what matters, and cherish every moment. Together, we can create a world filled with compassion and joy, one "Staffie smile" at a time.

As you turn the final page, carry Champ's light and legacy with you. Love never leaves us; it simply changes forms. The joy we shared with Champ will always be a part of us, inspiring and uplifting us daily. Hold on to the memories, embrace the lessons, and continue spreading the love Champ generously gave.

Thank you for being part of this journey. May you find peace, joy, and happiness in every moment, guided by Champ's spirit, as you unleash your true power. Give your furry pal an extra hug or pat, and tell them how much they mean to you.

The legacy of *Champ The Human Whisperer,* lives on in each of us.

Until we meet again... 🐾

With love and gratitude,
Dr. Harmony and Champ Avalon

CHAMP'S HEAVENLY MESSAGE: WISDOM FOR A HAPPIER LIFE

Hey there, Pawsome Person!

It's me, *Champ Avalon,* your angel dog from the rainbow bridge! Even though I've crossed over, my spirit is as strong as ever, and I'm here to share my tail-wagging wisdom with you. As you finish this book, I want to leave you with some final advice on how to live a doggone happy life, just like I did. Remember, this journey is only beginning—let's fetch some joy and make every day a *pawsome* adventure!

Here are my top tips for living your best life, straight from me, your angel dog:

- *When Loved Ones Come Home, Always Run to Greet Them.* Show your excitement and love; it makes everyone feel special.
- *Never Pass Up the Opportunity to Go for a Joyride.* Embrace new adventures and enjoy the ride, no matter where it takes you.
- *Allow the Experience of Fresh Air and the Wind in Your Face to Be Pure Ecstasy.* Savor the simple pleasures in life.
- *Take Naps.* Rest is important, so take time to recharge.
- *Stretch Before Rising.* A good stretch sets the tone for a great day.
- *Run, Romp, and Play Daily.* Keep your spirit lively and your body active.
- *Thrive on Attention and Let People Touch You.* Connect with others and share your love.
- *Avoid Biting When a Simple Growl Will Do.* Handle conflicts with grace.
- *On Warm Days, Stop to Lie on Your Back on the Grass.* Enjoy the beauty of nature.

- *On Hot Days, Drink Lots of Water and Lie Under a Shady Tree.* Stay cool and hydrated.
- *When You're Happy, Dance Around and Wag Your Entire Body.* Express your joy freely.
- *Delight in the Simple Joy of a Long Walk.* Appreciate the journey, not just the destination.
- *Eat with Gusto and Enthusiasm. Stop When You Have Had Enough.* Enjoy your meals and listen to your body.
- *Be Loyal. Never Pretend to Be Something You're Not.* Stay true to yourself.
- *If What You Want Lies Buried, Dig Until You Find It.* Pawsevere and never give up on your dreams.
- *When Someone Is Having a Bad Day, Be Silent, Sit Close By and Nuzzle Them Gently.* Offer comfort and support without words.
- *Be Always Grateful for Each New Day.* Start and end each day with gratitude.

I believe in you, my friend, you have the power to make a difference in your own life and the lives of those around you. Embrace the lessons we've shared, live with love and joy, and always wag your tail with enthusiasm. Life is an adventure, and every moment is a gift. Keep spreading happiness, and let your light shine as bright as the stars!

Until we meet again, keep wagging, keep smiling, and keep being *pawsome*—Staffie style! And don't forget to give your fur baby a big pat and hug—they too have lots to teach you.

High-paws and love always,
Champ Avalon 🐾

WHAT'S NEXT?
YOUR FREE MINI-COURSE

Unleash Your Inner Champ: The Power of Canine Wisdom

Now that you've completed *Champ The Human Whisperer: Unleashing the Wisdom of Man's Best Friend,* it's time to put *Champ's Timeless Tricks* into action. The journey doesn't end here—it's just beginning.

To help you transform your life, I'm offering a **special free mini-course, "Unleash Your Inner Champ: The Power of Canine Wisdom."** In this mini-course, you'll get a glimpse of the full **Strut Like Your Mutt** program by learning three key tricks that can help you reduce stress, find joy, and improve your relationships:

Free Mini-Course Outline:

1. **Shake Off the Stress**

   o **Lesson:** Dogs literally shake off stress after tense moments; you can too! Learn quick, effective techniques to reset your mind and let go of anxiety.
   o **Exercise:** Guided breathing and stress-shaking exercises.
   o **Takeaway:** Simple, actionable steps to help relieve stress in your daily routine.

2. **Play Like a Pup**

   o **Lesson:** Dogs find joy in simple play. Learn how to incorporate more fun and happiness into your life through playful activities.
   o **Exercise:** Create a personalized play plan for the week to reconnect with joy.
   o **Takeaway:** Boost your happiness by embracing small moments of fun.

3. **Love Unconditionally**

   o **Lesson:** Dogs love without judgment. Practicing empathy and unconditional love can enhance your relationships with others.

   o **Exercise:** Write a short gratitude note to someone you care about.

   o **Takeaway:** Strengthen your connections with appreciation and empathy.

Each part of this mini-course is designed to provide valuable insights and practical steps for integrating these lessons into your daily life.

How to Sign Up

Ready to get started? To access this **free mini-course**, visit www.strutlikeyourmutt.com or scan the QR code below to go directly to the sign-up page.

Continue the Journey with the Full Course

If you find value in these free lessons, the full **Strut Like Your Mutt** course is the next step to unlock all **8 Timeless Tricks** for living a more joyful, peaceful life. You'll dive deeper into each of Champ's tricks with practical exercises, personal stories, and transformative strategies.

Visit www.strutlikeyourmutt.com to sign up for the free preview. If you're ready for more, you can easily upgrade to the full course, with a portion of the proceeds going to support our mission and other affiliated organizations.

Thank you for being part of this journey with Champ and me. We look forward to seeing you in the training and continuing to spread joy, love, and wisdom together!

ACKNOWLEDGMENTS

To all the dogs who lost their lives simply because of their breed—you are not forgotten. Your stories inspire us to share our message, creating a world where love and understanding triumph over fear and prejudice. This book is a tribute to each of you.

To the no-kill shelters, rescues, volunteers, and foster parents who tirelessly work to save lives. Your dedication offers many hope, homes, and a second chance at life; your commitment and compassion light the way for change. You are a true hero, and I am endlessly grateful for all you do.

To everyone who supported Champ and me throughout our 100-Day Smile Challenge, your encouragement, love, and belief in Champ's mission gave us the strength to continue. To Champ's fans, followers, and the friends I've made through our shared love for dogs, thank you for walking this journey with us. The connections we've made transcend time and space, bound by the hearts of our beloved pets.

A special thank you to those who read and reviewed this book in advance. Your feedback and support have been invaluable in shaping this work. Your contribution has been instrumental in making this book a success.

And finally, to Lennox, a dog who lost his life because of breed discrimination. Your story touched the world and sparked a justice movement. This book stands as a voice for you and all pit bulls and bully breeds in solidarity with the advocates who tirelessly work to change the narrative.

Thank you all from the bottom of my heart. This book is a testament to our shared mission and a tribute to the dogs who have suffered due to breed discrimination. Let's continue to work towards a world where love and understanding triumph over fear and prejudice.

ABOUT DR. HARMONY

Best-Selling Author, Quantum Healer, and Transformational Mentor

Dr. Harmony is a world-renowned quantum healer, transformational mentor, best-selling author, and award-winning card deck creator. With over 30 years of experience in vibrational medicine and a background in chiropractic, she specializes in clearing energetic blockages, aligning spiritual energies, and empowering clients to manifest their highest potential. Her personalized healing approaches integrate advanced quantum techniques with intuitive guidance, fostering deep, transformative shifts for those seeking to align with their true essence.

Affectionately known as the "Mother Teresa of Canines," Dr. Harmony is also a passionate advocate for all dogs, particularly bully breeds. Her mission is to raise awareness and promote peace, freedom, and justice for these misunderstood and often mistreated animals. Inspired by her Staffordshire Bull Terrier and soulmate, Champ Avalon, Dr. Harmony has dedicated her life to creating a world where every dog is valued and loved.

In addition to her healing work, Dr. Harmony is the founder of *Soul Writers Academy,* where she helps aspiring authors discover their purpose and bring their stories to life. She guides others through planning, writing, and publishing their books, transforming their experiences into powerful messages of healing and inspiration.

You can follow Dr. Harmony on social media @TwinFlameExpert or visit SoulWritersAcademy.com to learn more about her work. For inquiries, contact her at info@SoulWritersAcademy.com.

ABOUT CHAMP AND THE BIRTH OF A MISSION

Meet Champ, a Staffordshire Bull Terrier who defied all odds, rising from the runt of his litter to become a symbol of hope and a proud ambassador for bully breeds. His unwavering loyalty, indomitable spirit, and infectious 'Staffie smile' shattered stereotypes and championed a powerful message of love, unity, and acceptance that resonates with all of us. His deep bond with Dr. Harmony helped her navigate personal healing while he imparted valuable lessons in mindfulness, emotional well-being, and overcoming life's challenges.

Together, they founded *Global Paws for Peace,* inspiring unity and kindness among all dogs and humans. Through this book, you'll explore Champ's remarkable journey and his shared wisdom, offering insights on living with purpose, finding inner peace, and embracing joy. From overcoming adversity to learning how to let go of stress, *Champ's timeless teachings*—like mindfulness techniques, intuition, and positive thinking—are here to transform your life.

With a blend of humor, dog language, and Champ's unique messages, this book takes you on a journey that is not just engaging but also deeply relatable. It underscores the profound healing power of the human-canine bond. Whether you're seeking stress relief, emotional healing, or a reminder of life's simple joys, *Champ The Human Whisperer* is your guide to living a life that is full and authentic.

Let Champ's journey inspire you to tap into your inner strength, spread kindness, and live with a wagging tail and an open heart. This book is not just a celebration of one incredible dog's legacy but an invitation to awaken your own inner Champ.

If you found this message helpful and would like to pay forward a copy of the book, it is available on Amazon. A portion of all proceeds supports our organization. You can also purchase the digital version directly from our website, where proceeds help fund our mission.

For more information on becoming an affiliate, where a portion of the proceeds benefits your organization, email us at info@GlobalPawsForPeace.org.

Scan the QR code below to learn more or to share the book:

ABOUT GLOBAL PAWS FOR PEACE AND THE 100-DAY SMILE CHALLENGE

A Legacy Love and Happiness

Dr. Harmony believes in "paying it forward," a principle that led her to establish *Global Paws for Peace.* This initiative aims to educate the public about bully breeds and advocate for their rights. A pivotal moment in her journey was the *100-Day Smile Challenge,* where she and Champ set out to make 100 people smile in 100 days. This challenge not only raised awareness about the loving nature of bully breeds but also aligned Dr. Harmony with her soul's purpose, fostering a life of joy and fulfillment. Champ's presence during this challenge became a metaphor for the impact of kindness and the importance of spreading joy.

Dr. Harmony's journey with Champ has been one of profound transformation. His legacy continues to inspire her mission to create unity among all breeds and promote the message of unconditional love and acceptance. Through *Global Paws For Peace* and her work, she strives to help others discover their inner strength, embrace their true purpose, and live a life filled with joy and compassion.

To get involved further, visit our website and follow us on social media for updates on events and volunteer opportunities. Your help can spread our message of love and unity even further.

Visit GlobalPawsForPeace.org or scan the QR code below:

177

Made in the USA
Columbia, SC
24 October 2024

44442844R00107